Counseling
and the
Nature of Man

DATE DUE

Counseling
and the
Nature of Man

Frank B. Minirth
and
Paul D. Meier

Baker Book House
Grand Rapids, Michigan 49506

Copyright 1982 by
Baker Book House Company

ISBN: 0–8010–6135–0

Printed in the United States of America

Unless indicated otherwise, Scripture quotations are from the New International Version, copyright 1978 by the New York International Bible Society. Other translations cited are the King James Version (KJV) and the New American Standard Bible (NASB) copyrighted by the Lockman Foundation, 1960, 1962, 1963, 1968, 1971, 1972, 1973, 1975, 1977.

Contents

Introduction

The need to maintain physical health has long been recognized. In the United States there are over one hundred medical schools, each turning out approximately one hundred doctors yearly. We are encouraged to have at least one physical examination annually. Literally billions of dollars are spent each year on professional medical services.

During the last hundred years, maintaining mental health has also become a matter of concern. Millions of dollars are spent annually on mental health. Professional interest in the subject has increased to such an extent that at present there are over 250 schools of psychotherapy.

The Christian is also interested in a third dimension—that of spiritual health. Adam, the first man, knew the importance of a close walk with God. Later, the wise king Solomon noted that there is a correlation between spiritual health (which can be ours if we abide by the Word of God) and general well-being.

What about considering the physical, mental, and spiritual dimensions together? Is not man one unit? Do not the dimensions affect one another? Indeed they do, and the relationships between them are a major theme of this book. Lately there has been an upsurge of interest in holistic medicine in general,[1] but very little has been written on integrating physical and psychological data with standard evangelical beliefs. To begin to fill in that gap is one of our aims.

In chapter 1 we concentrate on man's spiritual condition

1. Milton Chatton and Marcus Krupp, *Current Medical Diagnosis and Treatment* (Los Altos, CA: Lange Medical Publications, 1981), pp. 603–56. See also Jerome D. Frank, "Holistic Components of Illness and Healing," *Weekly Psychiatry Update Series* 2, Lesson 18 (Princeton, NJ: Biomedia, 1978).

without Christ—he is lost, incomplete, and vulnerable to Satan's attacks. Chapter 2 discusses the holistic nature of man—he is a physical, psychological, and spiritual creature, and all of these dimensions are integrally interrelated. The counselor must not focus on one to the neglect of the others. The highly complicated procedure of properly diagnosing a psychological problem is the subject of chapter 3, while chapter 4 describes a number of defense mechanisms which inhibit dealing with conflicts and frustrations in a healthy way and suggests Christian alternatives which the counselor can propose to his clients. Chapter 5 introduces what we designate the "Christian eclectic approach." The wise counselor makes use of the best methods of various major schools of psychotherapy. At the same time the Word of God remains his chief resource. In chapter 6 we explore the spiritual and psychological aspects of several key topics, including anxiety, guilt, and anger. A summary of skills which the Christian counselor must develop is presented in chapter 7. Finally, in chapter 8 we tie everything together, emphasizing once again the main points which the counselor must bear in mind if he is to be successful.

Man Without Christ

Man Without Christ Is Lost

If the counselor is going to be of any practical help to his clients, he must begin with a thorough knowledge of the nature of man. Fundamental to understanding the nature of man is the realization that man without Christ is lost. To ignore a counselee's eternal destiny while helping him to solve his present problems is utterly illogical. Man without Christ is lost (John 14:6) and eternally doomed to a literal hell (Matt. 10:28; 2 Thess. 1:9). Knowledge of that fact must underlie the whole counseling process. Compelled by the love of Christ (2 Cor. 5:14), the Christian counselor desires to see the counselee come to salvation by simply trusting that Christ died for his sins (John 1:12; Rom. 6:23). Surely nothing has ever offered greater potential for solving problems and resolved more conflicts than has freely accepting what Christ has done (John 6:37; Eph. 2:8–9). The Christian counselor earnestly hopes that each of his clients will one day be as open to receiving Christ as was Charlotte Elliott when she wrote:

> Just as I am, without one plea,
> But that Thy blood was shed for me,
> And that Thou bidd'st me come to Thee,
> O Lamb of God, I come! I come!
>
> Just as I am, and waiting not
> To rid my soul of one dark blot,
> To Thee whose blood can cleanse each spot,
> O Lamb of God, I come! I come!

> Just as I am, though tossed about
> With many a conflict, many a doubt,
> Fightings and fears within, without,
> O Lamb of God, I come! I come!

> Just as I am, Thou wilt receive,
> Wilt welcome, pardon, cleanse, relieve;
> Because Thy promise I believe,
> O Lamb of God, I come! I come!

Man Without Christ Is Incomplete

Not only is man lost without Christ, he is also incomplete. When left to himself man faces many conflicts and an existential loneliness. He lacks the deepest comfort and most powerful resource in the universe for solving problems—Jesus Christ. When one trusts Christ as his Savior, the Holy Spirit comes to indwell (1 Cor. 3:16), empower (Eph. 3:16), guide (Rom. 8:14), teach (John 14:26), and free from sin and death (Rom. 8:2). Upon receiving Christ as Savior, man literally has the resources of God Himself available for living life (John 15:4–7) and coping with his problems (1 Peter 5:7). The negative impact of conflicts will be greatly reduced as one learns to walk closely with God. Among biblical examples of men who benefited immeasurably from a close walk with God are Moses (Exod. 33), Hezekiah (2 Kings 18), Asaph (Ps. 73), and the apostle Paul (Phil. 3). Our overwhelming need for Christ to bring a sense of completion to our lives has been well expressed in an old hymn by Annie S. Hawks and Robert Lowry:

> I need Thee every hour,
> Most gracious Lord;
> No tender voice like Thine
> Can peace afford.

> I need Thee every hour,
> Stay Thou near by;
> Temptations lose their power
> When Thou art nigh.

I need Thee every hour,
In joy or pain;
Come quickly and abide,
Or life is vain.

I need Thee every hour,
Most Holy One;
O make me Thine indeed,
Thou blessed Son.

I need Thee, O I need Thee;
Every hour I need Thee!
O bless me now, my Savior,
I come to Thee!

Psychiatric research indicates that, if a child is to be healthy, he must feel that his parents will meet his dependency needs and never reject him. Certainly the same holds true for a child in the family of God. Understanding that man has certain dependency needs which only God can be expected to meet will have a large bearing on the counseling process.

Jane was a young woman thirty years of age who was experiencing depression as a result of marital conflicts. She did not know Christ and had no human resources to whom she could turn. She had become desperate and was considering suicide. But during a course of therapy she came to trust Christ. She began to receive support from the body of Christ. Many situational problems continued. However, she could now withstand the stress from without because Christ was within. In her own words, "I accepted Jesus Christ as my Lord and Savior after being hospitalized twice for depression and anxiety. In the past I had refused to look inward and acknowledge my self-centeredness. I made impossible demands of my loved ones in order that I might achieve happiness. But a person can love with a Christlike nature only from a secure position of accepting himself and others for what they are, as they are."

Man Is Depraved

Closely tied in with man's lostness and incompleteness without Christ is the fact that man is depraved. He is not basically good.

Although he may have some consciousness of right and wrong (Rom. 2:14-15), may not be as sinful as he could be (2 Tim. 3:13), and may perform some good works (Isa. 64:6), he is still depraved. There is no human being who is without sin (Rom. 3:9-20); man has an innate tendency to evil (Rom. 7:14-25), and, of course, can never satisfy God though he may attempt to establish his own righteousness (Rom. 10:1-4). Even after he accepts Christ he is still depraved. Although he now has a new nature, he is still being pulled toward sin by the dangerous old nature (Rom. 7:20; Gal. 5:17; Eph. 4:22-24).

The counselor who recognizes that man is by nature depraved knows that attempts at "self-actualization" will ultimately fail. That is, man in himself has neither the capability nor the goodness necessary to solve his own problems and overcome the evil within him. The Christian counselor agrees with Jeremiah's assessment that "the heart is more deceitful than all else and is desperately sick; who can understand it?" (Jer. 17:9, NASB). The mind is dishonest and tricky. Man employs various defense mechanisms in efforts to avoid taking an honest look at himself (see chapter 4).

Rationalization is one of the more common defense mechanisms. For example, an individual may declare, "I simply don't love my mate anymore. Surely God doesn't want me to stay in a marriage with someone I don't love." Actually the individual may be having an affair and trying to find a plausible excuse for his behavior. He is entangled in sin. The Christian counselor will ever be aware that depravity is an integral part of the nature of man.

Man Is Under Attack

Not only is man lost, incomplete, and depraved, but he is under constant attack by a most powerful enemy—Satan. Satan is more powerful, clever, and shrewd than most people realize. C. S. Lewis captured some of the craftiness of Satan most effectively in his best-selling *Screwtape Letters*.

Satan desires that nonbelievers stay in spiritual darkness (John 3:19-21). He also prowls about seeking to destroy the mental health of Christians (Eph. 6:11-16; 1 Peter 5:8-9). There are various devices Satan uses to accomplish these purposes. He can deceive, enticing people to pay attention to false doctrines (1 Tim. 4:1–3). He can influence thinking, causing man to focus on his own interests rather than on God's (Matt. 16:21–23). Satan can hinder the spread of the gospel (1 Thess. 2:2, 14–16). He can tempt (1 Cor. 7:5). He can oppress people mentally, even to the point of driving them insane (Luke 8:26–39). But although demonic possession is possible, Satan usually chooses to work in far more subtle ways. For example, he best accomplishes his purposes with Christians by tempting them over and over in the area of their greatest weakness, be it materialism, pride, lust, a tendency toward depression, or whatever. The great variety of Satan's schemes is, then, another factor of which the Christian counselor should be constantly aware.

The Holistic Nature of Man

Man has a holistic nature; that is, he is a physical, psychological, and spiritual creature, and all of these dimensions are interrelated. That man is a physical creature with physical weaknesses is obvious. It has been said that man begins to die at birth. After the age of forty literally thousands of brain cells die daily. Man is constantly struggling against physical disease. What is not so obvious is that man's physical condition is integrally related with his psychological and spiritual condition. Man is a whole. What affects him physically affects him psychologically and spiritually as well. A physical disease can lead to psychological and/or spiritual problems—and vice versa. This chapter briefly explores ways in which the various dimensions of the holistic nature of man are interdependent.

Physical Problems Can Produce Emotional Problems

Man's physical condition has a direct bearing on his emotional health. For example, certain diseases as well as certain drugs intended to relieve physical problems can produce symptoms of depression. Among the diseases which can cause depression are viral illnesses (mononucleosis and pneumonia), endocrine disorders (hypothyroidism), cancer of the pancreas, and multiple sclerosis. Depression can also be an aftereffect of a variety of drugs, including major and minor tranquilizers, birth-control pills, diet pills, medication for high blood pressure, and alcohol. Symptoms of anxiety are also often interconnected with man's physical condition. Tenseness, trembling, and even panic can be induced by endocrine disorders (hyperthyroidism), hormone abnormalities (hypoglycemia), tumors (phenochromo-cytoma), and various drugs (caffeine, marijuana, LSD, PCP, amphetamines).

Psychosis or a loss of touch with reality is another emotional disturbance that may be rooted in physical problems. Among the diseases that may result in psychosis are porphyria, Wilson's disease, Huntington's chorea, endocrine disorders (hyperthyroid-ism), and tumors of the temporal lobe of the brain. In addition there are a great many drugs which can cause one to lose contact with reality. They include illegal drugs (amphetamines, cocaine, LSD, PCP, and marijuana); prescriptions designed to combat seizures, depression, Parkinson's disease, or tuberculosis; alcohol; and even over-the-counter medications (nasal sprays, bromide-containing compounds to relieve anxiety, and sleeping pills).

It should also be mentioned that certain physical problems can produce changes in personality. Most notable in this connec-tion is the problem of senility. (See Figure 1 for an extensive list of physical conditions which can lead to emotional problems.)

Figure 1

Physical Causes of Psychological Problems*

1. Physical causes of depression.
   a. Viral illnesses—mononucleosis, pneumonia.
   b. Endocrine disorders—hypothyroidism, Cushing's syndrome, Addison's disease.
   c. Electrolyte abnormalities—hypermagnesemia.
   d. Other diseases—multiple sclerosis, cancer of the pancreas, dementia, rheumatoid arthritis.
   e. Endogenous depression (biochemical, genetically induced depression).
   f. "Masked depression" (this condition is characterized by physical complaints [such as headaches] which seem to have no organic pathology).
   g. Drugs—both prescription drugs (Valium; medication for high blood pressure, birth control, psychosis) and illegal drugs (amphetamines).
   h. Alcohol.

2. Physical causes of anxiety.
   a. Tumors—phenochromocytoma.
   b. Mitral-valve prolapse (this is the underlying problem in 30 to 40 percent of patients suffering from feelings of panic).
   c. Endocrine abnormalities—hyperthyroidism.
   d. Electrolyte abnormalities—hypomagnesemia, hypercalcemia (breast cancer).
   e. Hormone abnormalities—hypoglycemia (a temporary tense feeling and tremor follow the release of adrenalin).
   f. Dementia (chronic organic brain syndrome) or delirium (acute organic brain syndrome).
   g. Other diseases—vestibular disease, basilar-artery disease.

*This figure, like several others in this book, while extensive, is not intended to be exhaustive.

Physical Causes of Psychological Problems (Cont.)

    h. Hyperactivity.
    i. Drugs—caffeine (more than 500 milligrams or four to five cups of coffee per day), prescription drugs (minor tranquilizers; medication for depression or psychosis can induce tremors), and illegal drugs (amphetamines, marijuana, LSD, and PCP can cause panic).
    j. Alcohol (withdrawal, delirium tremens).

3. Physical causes of psychosis.
    a. Tumors, especially of the limbic system (psychosis occurs in 5 percent of the cases of temporal-lobe tumors).
    b. Endocrine abnormalities—hypothyroidism, hyperthyroidism.
    c. Other diseases—Huntington's chorea, porphyria, Wilson's disease.
    d. Head trauma.
    e. Drugs—prescription drugs (atropine; medication to combat seizures [Dilantin], depression, Parkinson's disease, tuberculosis, alcoholism [Antabuse]), over-the-counter drugs (nasal sprays, bromide-containing compounds to relieve anxiety, sleeping pills), and illegal drugs (amphetamines, cocaine, LSD, PCP, marijuana).
    f. Alcohol—Krosakoff's psychosis.

4. Physical causes of personality changes (e.g., accentuation of basic characteristics or release of inhibitions).
    a. Viral illnesses—Creutzfeldt-Jakob syndrome.
    b. Temporal-lobe epilepsy.
    c. Other diseases—multiple sclerosis, systemic lupus erythematosus.
    d. Trauma ("punch drunk").
    e. Senility.
    f. Drugs—marijuana (amotivational syndrome), LSD, PCP.
    g. Alcohol.

5. Physical causes of obsessive-compulsive disorder (repeated stereotyped behavior).
    a. Temporal-lobe epilepsy.
    b. Drugs—amphetamines.

6. Physical causes of apathy.
    a. Tumor of the right hemisphere of the brain.
    b. Other diseases—Alzheimer's disease, Pick's disease, normal-pressure hydrocephalus.
    c. Trauma.
    d. Alcohol—Wernicke's syndrome.

7. Physical causes of violence.
    a. Temporal-lobe epilepsy.
    b. Drugs—amphetamines, LSD, PCP.
    c. Alcohol.

8. Physical causes of abnormal religious preoccupation.
    a. Temporal-lobe epilepsy.
    b. Manic-depressive psychosis.
    c. Drugs.

9. Physical causes of amnesia.
    a. Cardiovascular accident.
    b. Trauma.
    c. Alcohol.

10. Physical causes of insomnia.
    a. Sleep apnea.
    b. Myoclonic jerks.
    c. Various medical diseases.
    d. Drugs—caffeine, amphetamines.

Physical Causes of Psychological Problems (Cont.)

11. Physical cause of hyperactivity (impulsiveness, distractibility, lack of concentration, poor school performance, behavior problems)—underdevelopment of the nervous system.

12. Physical causes of confusion.
   a. Degenerative diseases—Alzheimer's disease, Pick's disease.
   b. Vascular-circulatory disorders with relative ischemia—arrhythmias, congestive heart failure, repeated emboli and infarcts.
   c. Viral infections—encephalitis, chronic meningitis, herpes, influenza, measles, mumps.
   d. Chronic metabolic encephalopathy—endocrine abnormalities (hypoglycemia), circulatory disturbances (hypoxia).
   e. Tumors.
   f. Dementia or delirium.
   g. Other diseases—multiple sclerosis, normal-pressure hydrocephalus, septicemia, viremia, Parkinson's disease.
   h. Trauma—concussion, subdural hemorrhage.
   i. Nutritional deficiencies—lack of thiamine, niacin, vitamin B_{12}.
   j. Drugs—steroids, bromides, barbiturates, lithium, opiates, antibiotics, anticholinergics including over-the-counter sleep medications.
   k. Alcohol.
   l. Mental retardation (in this case apparent confusion is actually inability to understand).

Emotional Problems Can Produce Physical Problems

While physical problems can cause emotional problems, the reverse also holds true. For example, stress seems to result in a general predisposition to illness. It can lead to various psycho-physiologic diseases (ulcers, colitis, high blood pressure). Persons who lead stressful lives and feel pressured by the constraints of time are prone to coronary artery disease. Of utmost importance is the fact that stress can deplete the neurotransmitters in the brain (norepinephrine, serotonin, dopamine) and thus in turn produce depression or psychosis. Stress can also slow the speed of recovery from infectious disease or surgery. Loneliness may be an important factor in both the development of coronary artery disease and susceptibility to certain forms of cancer. In addition, studies have shown that in the first year after the death of a close relative, there is a sevenfold increase in the mortality rate. (See Figure 2 for an extensive outline of ways in which emotions influence the body.)

Figure 2

Emotional Factors with Physical Consequences

Unresolved emotional and spiritual problems can produce a host of physical problems. On the other hand, emotional well-being can promote physical health. Some of the more noteworthy ways in which emotions influence the body are suggested in the following outline.

1. When we are deprived of intimacy with others, our physical condition suffers.
   a. In the first year after the death of a close relative, there is a sevenfold increase in the mortality rate (this is the conclusion of studies comparing the recently bereaved with the general population).
   b. A young child separated from his mother for a prolonged period may fail to thrive and eventually die (anaclitic depression).
   c. Research has shown that loneliness may be an important factor in both the development of coronary artery disease and susceptibility to cancer.
2. The presence of emotional stress has enormous (largely detrimental) effects on physical health.
   a. Stress seems to result in a general predisposition to illness. It can also slow the speed of recovery from infectious diseases or surgery.
   b. By virtue of the interplay between the psychological, nervous, and endocrine systems, stress can lower our resistance to infection:

stress

↓

depletion of norepinephrine

↓

irregularity in the secretion
of hypothalamic-releasing factors

↓

change in the release of hormones
from the pituitary gland (e.g.,
growth hormones, luteinizing
hormones, thyroid-stimulating
hormone, adrenocorticotrophic
hormone, prolactin

↓

disturbances in endocrine glands

↓	↓
lowered resistance to physical diseases, including colds, pneumonia, cancer	increase in cortisol ↓ increase in liver enzymes which deplete serotonin and norepinephrine (we have come full circle back to the beginning of the process)

Another possible result of the depletion of norepinephrine due to stress is physical and biochemical depression.
   c. Stress plays a role in psychophysiologic diseases as well. Note once again the various parts of the body affected in the process.

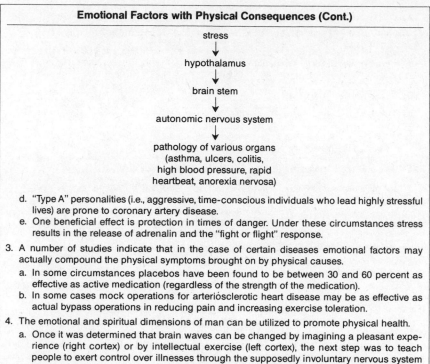

Emotional Factors with Physical Consequences (Cont.)

stress
↓
hypothalamus
↓
brain stem
↓
autonomic nervous system
↓
pathology of various organs
(asthma, ulcers, colitis,
high blood pressure, rapid
heartbeat, anorexia nervosa)

    d. "Type A" personalities (i.e., aggressive, time-conscious individuals who lead highly stressful lives) are prone to coronary artery disease.

    e. One beneficial effect is protection in times of danger. Under these circumstances stress results in the release of adrenalin and the "fight or flight" response.

3. A number of studies indicate that in the case of certain diseases emotional factors may actually compound the physical symptoms brought on by physical causes.

    a. In some circumstances placebos have been found to be between 30 and 60 percent as effective as active medication (regardless of the strength of the medication).

    b. In some cases mock operations for arteriosclerotic heart disease may be as effective as actual bypass operations in reducing pain and increasing exercise toleration.

4. The emotional and spiritual dimensions of man can be utilized to promote physical health.

    a. Once it was determined that brain waves can be changed by imagining a pleasant experience (right cortex) or by intellectual exercise (left cortex), the next step was to teach people to exert control over illnesses through the supposedly involuntary nervous system (biofeedback). By the use of tension-sensitive instruments with graphic readouts, people have learned to control tension headaches, nocturnal tooth grinding, and cardiac arrhythmias. It is also possible to lower the heart rate, the respiration rate, oxygen consumption, and blood pressure.

    b. By sharing our faith and instilling hope we have seen many of our patients experience complete remission from what may have appeared to be physical problems.

Physical and Emotional Problems Can Affect
Spiritual Life

Another indication that the various dimensions of man's nature are inextricably interrelated is the fact that certain physical and emotional problems have real or apparent effects on one's spiritual life. Individuals with temporal-lobe epilepsy may experience a renewed interest in religion and display a moral piety. Someone on the brink of a psychotic breakdown may be preoccupied by religious matters. A person with an obsessive-compulsive neurosis may fear that he has committed the un-pardonable sin or that he does not have a sufficient trust in Christ. Manic-depressives may talk in a religious jargon. While schizophrenics and multiple personalities may be thought to be demon-possessed, they are not. Proof of this is their response to antipsychotic medication. (See Figure 3 for a list of physical and emotional factors which affect spiritual life.)

Figure 3

Physical and Emotional Factors with Spiritual Consequences

There are a number of physical and emotional factors which have real or apparent effects on spiritual life:

1. *Temporal-lobe epilepsy* may result in heightened religious interest and perfectionistic ten-dencies. Individuals with temporal-lobe epilepsy may go from church to church, considering none of them good enough. In this case the problem is physical rather than spiritual.
2. *Drugs* have long been associated with "religious" experience.
3. *Defense mechanisms* such as denial, introjection, and projection may cause an individual to appear superreligious when in fact he is not.
4. *Psychosis* may involve a religious preoccupation. This is a result of an increase in abstract thinking rather than true spirituality.
5. *Manic-depressive disorder* causes some of its victims to talk in a religious jargon.
6. *Obsessive-compulsive neurosis* may involve constant worries that one is not saved or has committed the unpardonable sin. These worries mask the underlying conflicts (with one's parents or mate). There may also be a defect in the circuits of the central nervous system. The result is a religious obsession, an oppressive thought that cannot be dislodged. An apt comparison is a record player stuck in one groove.

Genetic Factors May Predispose to Psychological Problems

Finally, while we do not inherit psychological problems, it is possible to inherit a certain physical (genetic) makeup that may predispose us to certain psychological problems. There are a number of studies which support this contention. For example, schizophrenia occurs in only 1 percent of the general population. However, if one parent is schizophrenic, the risk rises to 10 percent. If both parents are schizophrenic, the risk is 50 percent. If a fraternal twin becomes schizophrenic, there is a 10-percent chance that the other will also. By contrast, if an identical twin becomes schizophrenic, there is a 50-percent chance that the other will also. This holds true even if they were separated at birth.

The occurrence of manic-depressive psychosis also provides evidence that there may be a physical predisposition to certain psychological problems. Close relatives of manic-depressives are twenty times more susceptible than is the general population. Studies of twins (including twins reared apart) give nearly irrefutable evidence that there is a genetic factor. Most striking is genetic-linkage research indicating that in certain types of manic-depressive psychosis the weakness is actually carried by X-chromosomes.

Moreover, various studies have shown that there may be a genetic weakness involved in many other cases of depression. For example, 30 percent of the victims have a family history of depression. If a fraternal twin suffers from depression, there is only about a 10-percent chance that the other will too. However, if the twins are identical, the risk jumps to 76 percent. Even if they were reared apart, the risk runs as high as 67 percent. The data are overwhelming. While it would be wrong to conclude that mental disorders are inherited, a genetic weakness which predisposes to certain psychological conditions is inherited. That weakness may be manifested under stress. (Figure 4 summarizes research studies indicating that some psychological problems may be genetically related.)

Figure 4

Genetic Factors in Psychological Problems

Genetic factors may make us vulnerable to certain mental problems. While, in general, people do not inherit mental problems, each of us inherits a certain biochemical and physiologic makeup. This makeup may predispose certain individuals, when they encounter stressful situations, to manifest symptoms (e.g., hallucinations, sleep disturbance) of various disorders. Research studies indicate that an inherited physical (genetic) weakness may make some families susceptible to specific psychological problems:

1. **Schizophrenia** occurs in only about 1 percent of the general population, but Kallman and Kety have discovered that the risk is much higher if one has a close relative who has suffered from the disorder:
    a. One parent—10 percent risk.
    b. Both parents—50 percent.
    c. Sibling—10 percent.
    d. Fraternal twin—10 percent.
    e. Identical twin—50 percent. This holds whether the twins were raised together or apart. If an adopted twin suffers from the disorder, there is a higher rate of schizophrenia among the biological relatives than among the adoptive family.

Genetic Factors in Psychological Problems (Cont.)

---

2. **Manic-depressive psychosis** occurs in about .5 percent of the general population, but studies by Kallman and Winokur have shown that the risk increases substantially if there is a close relative who has experienced psychosis:

   a. A parent or sibling—10 percent. In 80 percent of the cases of bipolar psychosis there is a family history.
   b. Fraternal twin raised in the same home—26 percent.
   c. Identical twin raised in the same home—66–96 percent.
   d. Identical twin raised separately—75 percent.

3. **Depression** also seems to occur relatively often in certain families. In 30 percent of the cases of depression there is a family history. As in other disorders, if one twin suffers, the risk to the other twin is high:

   a. Fraternal twin—7–29 percent.
   b. Identical twin raised in the same home—60–76 percent.
   c. Identical twin raised separately—44–67 percent.

4. **Alcoholism,** according to Goodwin, may in some cases (particularly in males) be a genetic problem related to acid aldehyde.

5. **Sociopathy,** according to the research of Hutchings, involves both genetic and environmental factors.

Man, then, is physical, and yet man is far more than physical. He also has psychological and spiritual dimensions, and all of these dimensions are intertwined. Man has a holistic nature. Physical disease can result in psychological symptoms, psychological stress can produce physical disease, and spiritual problems in many cases lie at the core of or are caused by physical and/or emotional conditions.

Consider the case of an active church officer who was referred to us by his pastor. This church officer was a godly man who had given years of dedicated service to the church. One day he suddenly began to use obscene language and to make sexual advances toward nearly every woman with whom he came in contact. At the same time he talked more and more about spiritual matters. Thus he seemed to be overtly involved in sin one minute and to be superreligious the next. Was his problem spiritual, psychological, or perhaps even physical? During the course of our evaluation we discovered that he was suffering from a specific type of seizure that has not only physical, but also psychological and spiritual manifestations. Given proper medical treatment for the seizure, he was able to return to a normal life.

3

The Diagnosis of
Psychological Problems

If the counselor is to treat a psychological problem successfully, he must first make a proper diagnosis. This is a highly complicated procedure. The counselor begins by observing the client closely for symptoms that provide clues to the precise nature of the problem. Careful evaluation of these observations will help the counselor to pinpoint the difficulty. Then he must probe to find the root cause of the problem; often this entails conflicts which reach back into the counselee's early childhood. Only after the counselor has observed the client closely, evaluated the symptoms, identified the problem, and discovered the root cause can he prescribe suitable treatment. In this chapter we will consider the several aspects of this diagnostic procedure.

Observing Symptoms

It must be understood from the start that there is a virtually unlimited spectrum of psychological problems, each of them manifesting a variety of symptoms. Some symptoms are so bizarre that anyone could recognize them. Others are so subtle that the most trained observer may miss them. The counselor must closely note the client's dress, general behavior, actions, gestures, facial expressions, moods, and basic attitudes. There are also a number of questions to be asked: Is the counselee introverted or extroverted? aggressive or shy? sensitive or insensitive? active or passive? tense or calm? euphoric or sad? intense or frivolous? warm or cold? disciplined or impulsive? hostile or tolerant? suspicious or trusting? dominant or submissive? Is the

23

client in touch with reality? Does he have insight and sound judgment?

Identifying the Problem

By piecing together and carefully evaluating the various symptoms which have been observed over an appropriate period of time, the counselor will be able to identify the particular psychological problem. (See Figure 5 for brief characterizations of a large number of mental disorders.) If the counselee has exhibited unwarranted anxiety, obsessive worry, fear, or depression for several months, then by definition he has a neurosis. In general, each type of long-standing personality disorder is characterized by a variety of telltale signs. For example, the paranoid personality is overly suspicious and critical, easily feels slighted, lacks warmth, and takes pride in his ability to view things objectively. The compulsive personality is characterized by perfectionism, workaholism, inability to relax, stubborn determination, rigidity, and extreme feelings of guilt. The hysterical individual is emotional, dramatic, and attention-seeking. Dependent and demanding, he is manipulative and seductive with others. Many hysterical individuals go through a series of love affairs. Inefficiency, forgetfulness, procrastination, pouting, and a general passivity are marks of the passive-aggressive individual. Antisocial personalities are frequently in conflict with the rest of society (parents, siblings, mate, children, school, work, and the law). The schizoid individual has few, if any, friends; often exhibiting bizarre behavior, he may experience delusions or hallucinations.

Of course, everyone exhibits many of the symptoms we have just mentioned. That is part of being human. It is only when these symptoms are present to an extreme degree that they cause problems. Recognition that these symptoms (as well as various defense mechanisms—see chapter 4) occur among Christians is vital to the counselor who works with church groups. The wise counselor will be aware of any dominant traits within a group and adjust his approach accordingly. For example, he will be very cautious in dealing with a group of people who are hypercritical of others and proud of their cold objectivity.

In working with a church group which tends to be overly emotional, the counselor will put an added stress on doctrine. On the other hand, in working with a group that seems overly intellectual, he will emphasize the love and grace of Christ.

Figure 5

Characteristics of Mental Disorders*

1. Psychoses.
   a. *Schizophrenia* is a severe mental disorder characterized by the "four A's" (flat [nonexpressive] affect, loose associations, ambivalence, and autism), bizarre behavior, hallucinations and/or delusions.
   b. *Brief reactive psychosis* follows a stressful event and lasts less than two weeks.
   c. *Atypical psychosis* is also short-lived, but, unlike brief reactive psychosis, cannot be traced to any known cause of stress.
   d. *Schizoaffective disorder* is marked by both schizophrenic and affective symptoms.

2. Neuroses.
   a. *Anxiety neurosis* is characterized by free-floating tension and worry.
   b. *Phobia* is irrational fear.
   c. *Obsessive-compulsive neurosis* involves anxieties which develop after a traumatic event.
   d. *Somatoform disorder (Briquet's syndrome)* involves multiple somatic complaints which are secondary to anxiety.
   e. *Psychogenic-pain disorder* is marked by complaints of pain without a physical cause.
   f. *Hypochondriasis* is an obsessive fear that one has a serious disease.

3. Personality disorders.
   a. *Paranoid personalities* are suspicious and hypersensitive, and project their own faults onto others.
   b. *Obsessive-compulsive personalities* desire to control themselves and others, and fall into the traps of workaholism and perfectionism.
   c. *Hysterical personalities* are emotional, excitable, and exhibitionistic.
   d. *Passive-aggressive personalities* are prone to procrastination, forgetfulness, and stubbornness.
   e. *Passive-dependent personalities* have such a low degree of self-confidence that they allow others to assume responsibility.
   f. *Sociopathic personalities* have a problem of self-identity, demonstrating instability in their moods and friendships.
   g. *Narcissistic personalities* have a long-standing, grandiose preoccupation with self.
   h. *Schizoid personalities* are characterized by aloofness.
   i. *Avoidant personalities* desire but shun social relationships because of a hypersensitivity to rejection.
   j. *Schizotypal personalities* occasionally manifest very eccentric, almost psychotic behavior.
   k. *Cyclothymic personalities* are characterized by alternating moods (from high to low).
   l. *Dysthymic personalities* display a depressed mood.

4. Substance abuse.
   The abuse of drugs results in physical addiction and social complications.

5. Organic mental disorders.
   a. *Dementia* is a progressively severe brain disorder characterized by disorientation and impairment of intellectual functions.

*This outline of mental disorders is largely dependent on the *Diagnostic and Statistical Manual of Mental Disorders,* 3rd ed. (Washington, DC: American Psychiatric Association, 1978).

Characteristics of Mental Disorders (Cont.)

   b. *Delirium* is a state of clouded consciousness.
   c. *Organic amnestic syndrome* involves loss of memory.
   d. *Organic delusional syndrome* involves an irrational clinging to false beliefs.
   e. *Organic hallucinosis* causes one to see or hear things that are not really there.
   f. *Organic affective syndrome* is characterized by depression.
   g. *Organic personality syndrome* involves a distinct change from one's usual temperament.

6. Affective disorders.

   a. *Manic-depressive disorder* is marked by mood swings reaching psychotic levels.
   b. *Major depression* involves extreme symptoms (both psychological and physical) of depression.

7. Adjustment disorder.
   Maladaptive reactions (anxiety, depression, or withdrawal) to a specific stress often result in affective disorders.

8. Disorders appearing in early life (infancy, childhood, or adolescence).

   a. *Mental retardation* is subaverage intellectual functioning.
   b. *Attention-deficit disorder* is an inability to concentrate for more than a very limited period of time.
   c. *Conduct disorder* involves repeated patterns of antisocial behavior.
   d. *Anxiety disorder* is characterized by unwarranted tension and worry.
   e. *Identity disorder* is distress over a number of those elements by which one establishes himself as an individual (lifetime goals, career, friends, sex, sense of morality, religion, etc.).
   f. *Anorexia nervosa* is characterized by a drastic weight loss due to an intense fear of becoming fat.
   g. *Bulimia* is binge eating followed by forced vomiting.
   h. *Motor-tic disorder* involves recurrent, involuntary, purposeless movements, particularly of the eye or face.
   i. *Tourette's disorder* involves motor tics and multiple vocal tics.
   j. *Stuttering* is a spasmodic hesitation in speaking, or a repetition or prolongation of sounds or words.
   k. *Enuresis* is an involuntary voiding of urine.
   l. *Encopresis* is a voluntary or involuntary passing of feces at inappropriate times.
   m. *Infantile autism* is a gross and sustained impairment in social relationships which appears before the age of thirty months.
   n. *Specific developmental disorder* is a delay in the rate of learning a particular skill such as language, reading, or arithmetic.
   o. *Reactive attachment disorder* is characterized by poor emotional and physical development.
   p. *Elective mutism* is refusal to speak.
   q. *Oppositional disorder* is active or passive resistance to authority figures.

9. Impulse-control disorders.

   a. *Pathological gambling* is repeated engagement in betting to the point of social disruption.
   b. *Kleptomania* is an obsessive impulse to steal.
   c. *Pyromania* is an uncontrollable impulse to set fires.
   d. *Explosive disorder* involves repeated outbursts of aggression.

10. Sexual disorders.

   a. *Transsexualism* is an overwhelming desire to be the opposite sex.
   b. *Paraphilia* is sexual arousal in abnormal ways (fetishism, transvestism, zoophilia, pedophilia, exhibitionism, voyeurism, sadism, masochism).
   c. *Psychosexual dysfunction* covers a wide spectrum of problems, including inhibited sexual desire, frigidity, impotence, difficulties with orgasm, premature ejaculation, painful intercourse, and vaginismus.

Discovering the Root Cause

Once the counselor has evaluated the symptoms in order to identify the general nature of the problem, there is still a major task ahead—he must discover the root cause. As he proceeds, he must constantly keep in mind the holistic nature of man. Psychological problems are very often interconnected with the physical and spiritual dimensions of man. To be successful, the counselor must have an understanding of and an ability to deal with all of these aspects.

In most cases the roots of psychological problems lie in early childhood. Imagine the child's brain to be like a computer. The brain starts out essentially unprogramed, but by age six it has received extensive programing, particularly from parents. If the parents feed in faulty data (e.g., if they are possessive, harsh, cold, or overly permissive), the child's ability to respond appropriately to life and its crises may be permanently hindered. If the parents are frequently absent and thus fail to meet the child's dependency needs, he may later be prone to depression or sociopathy. If parents do not allow their child to be an individual, he may become schizophrenic. If parents are harsh, the child may eventually be guilt-ridden, compulsive, overly critical, paranoid, or sociopathic. If parents reward dramatic behavior, the child is likely to develop a hysterical personality. If parents are in constant conflict with each other, the likely result is deep-seated insecurity and anxiety (i.e., a neurosis) in the child. The possibilities are virtually inexhaustible.

After the root cause has been discovered, the counselor can initiate a program of treatment for the psychological problem. At this point the individuality of the client and his problem must be uppermost in the counselor's mind. Christ did not treat everyone the same; neither can the Christian counselor, for people are programed differently. One was never loved or accepted; another was smothered by love to the point of being overprotected. One was treated harshly; another was never disciplined. One had good role models; another did not. One watched his father develop ulcers; another watched his father explode in rage. One learned to get what he wants by aggressive behavior; another copes with his problems by being passive.

One does not know how to deal with his unresolved anger; another may even deny he has it.

By now the complexity of the diagnostic process should be apparent. The counselor must begin by closely observing the client for symptoms. Then he must gather together and carefully evaluate these clues in order to categorize the problem. Then he must dig through to the root cause, which more often than not is to be found in early childhood. Only at this point can the counselor prescribe a proper method of treatment. And throughout the whole process he must be conscious not only of the psychological dimension, but the physical and spiritual as well. Further, he must be aware of the individuality of the client, and hence of the individuality of the problem, the cause, and the treatment. Only with God's help can the counselor succeed in so monumental a task.

4

The Mechanisms of Defense

Psychological defense mechanisms are defined by Charles Morris as "the ways people react to frustration and conflict by deceiving themselves about their real desires and goals in an effort to maintain their self-esteem and avoid anxiety."[1] That standard secular textbook definition suggests a number of elements in a Christian interpretation of defense mechanisms.

A Christian Interpretation of Defense Mechanisms

Element 1

Defense mechanisms are automatic reactions to frustration and conflict. Our human brains automatically deceive us into viewing everyday conflicts and frustrations in a somewhat prejudiced way so that we can defend our false pride and put the blame for these conflicts on anyone other than ourselves.

Element 2

Defense mechanisms are unconscious, or beyond the awareness of the persons using them, since such persons deceive "themselves about their real desires and goals." The Bible says, "All a man's ways seem right to him, but the LORD weighs the heart" (Prov. 21:2). We humans self-righteously justify everything we do but God sees through us and uncovers the true desires and motives of our hearts. We often are not even aware of them, thanks to our self-deceiving defense mechanism.

1. Charles Morris, *Psychology: An Introduction* (Englewood Cliffs, NJ: Prentice-Hall, 1973), pp. 439–40.

Element 3

Defense mechanisms are sinful because all forms of deceit, including self-deceit, are sin. Solomon said, "The wisdom of the prudent is to give thought to their ways, but the folly of fools is deception" (Prov. 14:8). Wise, mature Christians take the time to analyze their own behavior. Some introspection is healthy. Foolish (immature) persons keep making the same mistakes in life because they don't make an effort to analyze prayerfully their own blind spots.

Element 4

The purpose of these automatic, unconscious, self-deceiving defense mechanisms is to maintain a false sense of self-esteem and to avoid anxiety. Anxiety is the fear of the unknown—the fear that we may become aware of some unacceptable desire or motive within ourselves that we really don't want to know, since it would produce increased guilt and decreased self-esteem. All human beings have some degree of inferiority feelings. Apart from the grace of God we all go through life unconsciously attempting to prove that we, as individuals, are significant. We deceive ourselves continually to protect ourselves from inner feelings of insignificance and guilt. The only true solution is faith in Jesus Christ for the total forgiveness of all of our past, present, and future sins, and a healthy realization that, in God's eyes, we *are* significant—significant enough for Him to adopt us into His family as His own sons and daughters and to give us eternal life.

Element 5

All people use defense mechanisms to deceive themselves in reaction to frustrations and conflicts. Even secular psychologists who naively believe in the basic goodness of humanity will readily admit, because of the overwhelming research data on defense mechanisms, that all humans are basically self-deceiving. Many psychologists, however, believe that defense mechanisms are good and should be encouraged to prevent insanity. It is true that these mechanisms frequently do prevent or delay insanity because the reality about our depraved desires and motives is extremely painful. An alternative is new birth in Christ, followed by progressive sanctification as we meditate on Scripture and gradually accept more and more of the truth about ourselves. Biblical solutions to the sinful motives and desires we find in ourselves will produce freedom from emotional pain. The truth will set us free, even though the truth hurts as we discover it. The only human who never used self-deceiving defense mechanisms is Jesus Christ, the God-man, whose self-esteem was valid and who had no sinful motives to become aware of.

Element 6

Awareness of the truth about ourselves does produce emotional pain (anxiety, guilt, and fear). Being around people who have psychological hangups similar to our own gives us a gut-level feeling of wanting to condemn or reject such people. Because they remind us unconsciously of ourselves, we become anxious. That anxiety is the root source of human prejudice. It is also the reason why insecure fathers feel more rejection toward their eldest sons, and insecure mothers toward their eldest daughters. The father becomes critical of his eldest son for the shortcomings the father possesses himself; likewise, the mother of her eldest daughter. Obviously, children model the behavior and attitudes of the parent of the same sex. Later, as teen-agers, they feel hostile toward their parents because the truth these teen-agers are hiding from themselves threatens to come to their awareness through their parents' guidance or discipline. If humans could accept the truth about themselves, and by the grace of God accept their own significance through Christ (in spite of their personal weaknesses), then all people would have genuine self-worth and there would be no conflicts between individuals or wars between nations. Scripture makes it plain, however, that nothing like that will happen until after the second coming of Jesus Christ.

Element 7

That human beings habitually and continually deceive themselves to maintain a false sense of self-esteem and to alleviate emotional pain reveals the truth that many human thoughts, desires, goals, and motives—on a deep inner level of consciousness—are selfish, destructive, or distorted. The key to understanding Christian psychology is found in Jeremiah 17:9: "The heart is deceitful above all things, and desperately wicked: who can know it?" (KJV). The human heart (mind, emotions, and will) is more deceitful than anything else in God's universe. It is so desperately wicked that we cannot even know it; we cannot understand the dimensions of human depravity. Even many of the good acts (humanly speaking) that humans do are done unconsciously for sinful motives (for example, to impress others or to deceive ourselves into thinking we are basically good). The apostle Paul had these comments about the basic lack of goodness in human nature.

> Furthermore, since they did not think it worthwhile to retain the knowledge of God, he gave them over to a depraved mind, to do what ought not to be done. They have become filled with every kind of wickedness, evil, greed and depravity. They are full of envy, murder, strife, deceit and malice. They are gossips, slanderers, God-haters, insolent, arrogant and boastful; they invent ways of doing evil; they disobey their parents; they are senseless, faithless, heartless, ruthless. Although they know God's righteous decree that those who do such things deserve death, they not only continue to do these very things, but also approve of those who practice them (Rom. 1:28–32).
>
> What shall we conclude then? Are we any better? Not at all! We have already made the charge that Jews and Gentiles alike are all under sin. As it is written:

> > There is no one righteous, not even one; there is no one who understands, no one who searches for God. All have turned away and together become worthless. There is no one who does good, not even one. Their throats are open graves; their tongues practice deceit. The poison of vipers is on their lips. Their mouths are full of cursing and bitterness. Their feet are swift to shed blood; ruin and misery mark their ways, and the way of peace they do not know. There is no fear of God before their eyes.

> Now we know that whatever the law says, it says to those who are under the law, so that every mouth may be silenced and the whole world held accountable to God. Therefore no one will be

declared righteous in his sight by observing the law; rather, through the law we become conscious of sin (Rom. 3:9–20).

For all have sinned and fall short of the glory of God (Rom. 3:23).

For the wages of sin is death, but the gift of God is eternal life through Christ Jesus our Lord (Rom. 6:23).

Moses wrote: "The LORD saw how great man's wickedness on the earth had become, and that every inclination of the thoughts of his heart was only evil all the time. The LORD was grieved that he had made man on the earth, and his heart was filled with pain" (Gen. 6:5–6).

We are blind to our own sinfulness. Solomon, who could have had any wish he wanted from God, chose God's offer of great wisdom and insight into human nature, so he could judge his people well. After counseling and judging thousands of people, Solomon said that "with much wisdom comes much sorrow; the more knowledge, the more grief" (Eccles. 1:18). Finding out the truth about human depravity is a painful process that brings temporary grief, partly because the more we learn about the depraved motives, desires, and defense mechanisms of humankind in general, the more we learn about our own. In the end, that knowledge can bring us joy and a greater acceptance of others. After all, who are we to condemn a person for being unrighteous when we are depraved ourselves? That would add hypocrisy to our already long list of conscious and unconscious sins. David the psalmist prayed intently that God would reveal David's own innermost thoughts, so he could daily be pleasing to the Lord (Ps. 139:23).

The apostle Paul encouraged Christians not only to examine themselves (2 Cor. 13:5), but also to faithfully confront other Christians because we love them (Eph. 4:15; 2 Tim. 4:1–5). Through Moses, God stated, "Rebuke your neighbor frankly so you will not share in his guilt. Do not seek revenge or bear a grudge against one of your people, but love your neighbor as yourself. I am the LORD" (Lev. 19:17–18).

The author of the Book of Hebrews offered the following encouragement: "Therefore, since we are surrounded by such a great cloud of witnesses, let us throw off everything that hinders

and the sin that so easily entangles, and let us run with per-
severance the race marked out for us. Let us fix our eyes on
Jesus, the author and perfecter of our faith . . ." (Heb. 12:1–2a).
Christians are to get rid of the sins in their lives and everything
else that hinders them from serving God. Undoubtedly that
would include childhood conflicts, hangups, and defense mechanisms. God enables us to do this gradually, to spare us the pain
of seeing ourselves as we really are all at once. Experienced
psychiatrists know that patients have to be stripped of their
defense mechanisms gradually; to do so rapidly might produce a
psychotic break to escape overwhelming emotional pain.

Scores of defense mechanisms that humans commonly use
have been described by psychiatrists and clinical psychologists.
No one uses all of them, but every individual uses many of them
daily. Certain mechanisms appear to predominate in people with
certain personality types. For example, the primary defense
mechanism of paranoid personalities is projection. Nearly everyone uses projection occasionally, but paranoid individuals use it
as their chief method of self-deceit and use it more often than
persons with other personality traits. Nearly all of the known
defense mechanisms, including projection, are described in
Scripture. Typical examples include Saul projecting his own
hostility onto David and David projecting his guilt over his sin
with Bathsheba to an imagined culprit who stole a neighbor's
only pet lamb. (For a thorough description of projection and
other defense mechanisms described in the Book of James, see
Melvin R. Nelson, "The Psychology of Spiritual Conflict," *Journal
of Psychology and Theology*, Winter, 1976, Vol. 1, No. 1, pages
34–41.)

Figure 6 identifies forty defense mechanisms and gives an
example of each.

Christian Alternatives to Defense Mechanisms

Christians as they grow toward Christlike maturity should
strive to become aware of and gradually do away with unconscious defense mechanisms. Thus, self-deceiving defenses can be
replaced with healthy defenses. Following is a list of some of the
healthy, scripturally acceptable defenses against emotional pain:

1. *Forgiveness.*   Forgiving others who have wronged you, or forgiving yourself when you have made a mistake or committed a sin, is the primary healthy, scriptural, and psychological defense against unhappiness and even clinical depression. Holding grudges is a primary cause of human depression. Christians are encouraged in Scripture to go ahead and get angry—without

---

Figure 6

Unconscious Defense Mechanisms Frequently Seen in Counseling

Name	Description	Example
1. Denial	Thoughts, feelings, wishes, or motives are denied access to consciousness. It is the primary defense mechanism of histrionic personalities, who deny their own sinful thoughts, feelings, wishes, or motives even when they become obvious to those around them.	A histrionic female behaves seductively but is not consciously aware of doing so because of denial, then becomes angry at the man she is unconsciously seducing for making sexually suggestive responses. Naivete can be a form of denial. (See also Prov. 14:15; 16:2.)
2. Distortion	Individuals grossly reshape external reality to suit their own inner needs, frequently including grandiose delusions, wish-fulfilling delusions, and hallucinations (for example, voices from "God" or "demons").	An extremely insecure individual who is flunking out of medical school uses distortion to protect himself from the pain of reality. He convinces himself that he will soon be asked to become president of the medical school because of his tremendous insights, and he hears God's voice several times per hour reassuring him of his delusions.
3. Delusional Projection	An individual who is so afraid of his own feelings, perhaps anger or lust, projects (like a slide projector on a screen) his feelings onto other persons in his environment, thus convincing himself that others are the possessors of those feelings and are plotting to use those feelings against him.	King Saul, unaware of the extent of his own extreme feelings of jealousy and hostility toward David when David became popular with the Israelites, developed the delusion that David was plotting to kill him. He projected his own wishes to murder David onto David (1 Sam. 18—31).
4. Primary Projection	The same as delusional projection but not of such psychotic proportions. Primary projection, used by nearly all persons, is the primary defense mechanism of paranoid personalities.	A person has strong cravings for attention but is unaware of them because such awareness would hurt his false pride. Being around other attention-seeking persons arouses his anxiety (fear of finding out the truth) level, so he self-righteously condemns the "mote" in his brother's eye instead of the "log" in his own (Matt. 7:1-5). See also Romans 2:1-3 and James 1:13-17.
5. Schizoid Fantasy	Individuals who find reality painful escape the pain of reality through excessive daydreaming.	A girl who is very shy and fearful of intimacy spends much time in schizoid fantasy about the perfect romance, but refuses to date the boys who ask her out because they do not measure up to the perfect man of her dreams. She may develop anger toward God for not providing her with a mate, when in reality she is unconsciously rejecting all men.

Unconscious Defense Mechanisms Frequently Seen in Counseling (Cont.)

Name	Description	Example
6. Isolation	Various unacceptable emotions (jealousy, greed, or lust) are split off from conscious thoughts and isolated from conscious awareness.	This mechanism is commonly used by compulsive individuals whose consciences are so strict that they mistakenly think all anger is sin (in contradiction to Eph. 4:26), so they isolate their anger to relieve their own false guilt. In reality they are sinning by deceiving themselves, not by experiencing the negative emotion of anger. God would have preferred for them to be aware of their anger so they could deal with the problem maturely and forgive the other person "by sundown." (See Eph. 4:26 and Lev. 19:17–18.)
7. Rationalization	Individuals justify unacceptable attitudes, beliefs, or behavior by the misapplication of justifying reasons or the invention of false reasons.	A pastor who spends an inordinate amount of time with a histrionic female counselee because of his own lustful thoughts toward her unconsciously convinces himself that his motives are pure. He rationalizes that he is seeing her out of "Christian love" because she needs to spend much time with a "father figure" to compensate for the father who ignored her as a child. (See Rom. 3:5–8 and Prov. 21:2.)
8. Reaction Formation	Attitudes and behavior are adopted that are opposite of an individual's true conscious or unconscious impulses.	A histrionic religious leader who harbors strong homosexual and/or heterosexual urges becomes an evangelist who preaches primarily against sexual promiscuity or sex education in schools. Periodically, however, he "falls into sin" and has affairs with women he meets on his evangelistic tours. Reaction formation is sometimes also called "antithetic counteraction." See Romans 2:28–29 and James 1:26–27 for related implications.
9. Repression	Unacceptable ideas, feelings, impulses, or motives are banished from conscious awareness; or unconscious ideas, feelings, impulses, or motives are prevented from coming into conscious awareness. All persons use repression, the most general defense mechanism. *Repression is the primary defense mechanism on which all other defense mechanisms are based.*	A Christian dying of cancer continually represses personal anger toward God for allowing the cancer to develop. Because the patient is repressing his true feelings he may feel insulted when a close friend asks him if his anger has caused him to lose interest in having personal devotions.
10. Unhealthy Suppression	Individuals indefinitely postpone dealing with a conscious conflict. The individuals suppress the truth by fooling themselves into thinking they will deal with the conflict later, but "later" never comes. This is actually a *semiconscious* defense mechanism.	The individuals described in Romans 1:18–32 incurred the wrath of God (v. 18) because they suppressed the truth about their sinful condition and need of a Savior, becoming instead progressively more sinful.

Unconscious Defense Mechanisms Frequently Seen in Counseling (Cont.)

Name	Description	Example
11. Phariseeism	Individuals become increasingly self-righteous (thinking themselves better than others because of what they do or don't do religiously) to avoid becoming aware of their own depravity.	A college student who has had lifelong unconscious inferiority feelings because of his own repressed selfishness and hostility becomes a Christian and feels "called by God" to preach. As a pastor he preaches consistently against committing "the dirty dozen" sins and feeds his flock a steady diet of legalism, thinking himself to be more righteous and holy than other, less legalistic Christians, whom he condemns as "instruments of the devil." Like the Pharisees in Christ's day, he loves to pray out loud with much verbosity, to preach long sermons, and to brag publicly about the shortness of his hair or some other "spiritual" qualification. See Luke 18:9–14 for an excellent example of Phariseeism.
12. Defensive Devaluation	Related to Phariseeism; individuals are continually critical of others to convince themselves that they are better than others. This is one of the main ways that nearly all persons cover up their unconscious inferiority feelings. It is related to projection.	Individuals using defensive devaluation are in reality unconsciously angry at themselves for not being perfect, but find it less threatening to continually criticize the imperfections of others who unconsciously remind them of their own imperfections. (See also James 2:1–9.)
13. Introjection	Individuals "introject" or symbolically "throw within themselves" or redirect toward themselves the feelings they have toward another person, or the feelings of another person. Introjection, the opposite of projection, has several dimensions. Young children use introjection to incorporate parental feelings and attitudes into their own egos as part of identification. Compulsive individuals may feel very angry at another person unconsciously, but to avoid guilt feelings may introject the anger toward themselves instead. This usually initiates physiological processes in their bodies that will eventually result in the physiological concomitants of depression.	A pastoral counselor may introject the depression of a counselee into himself, thus magically thinking that by taking on such suffering he will somehow relieve his counselee. In reality both counselee and counselor leave the session feeling painfully sad.

Unconscious Defense Mechanisms Frequently Seen in Counseling (Cont.)

Name	Description	Example
14. Passive-Aggressive Unconscious Behavior	Passive, dependent individuals who have repressed hostility toward an individual or institution on which they are dependent get unconscious revenge on that authority figure in nonverbal ways, such as pouting, procrastination, stubbornness, inefficiency, or obstructionism.	An alcoholic male represses his hostility toward a domineering, mothering, compulsive wife. He dares not express anger toward her or even be aware of it, so he gets even with her by coming home late from work, putting off daily chores, and eventually dying of liver disease. A more subtle example would be a passive-aggressive pastor who represses his anger toward the church leadership for two or three years but accumulates unconscious grudges toward them. He gets even with them surprisingly one day when he splits the entire church over a noncrucial issue. Many Scripture passages, such as Romans 2:5–6, deal with stubbornness and other passive-aggressive behaviors and attitudes.
15. Withdrawal	Individuals deceive themselves about the existence of a tension-producing conflict by removing themselves from the situation.	An introvert fears intimacy but denies to himself that he has that fear. He gets engaged three times but withdraws from each relationship when it gets close to marriage, not knowing consciously that his true reason for breaking up was his own fear of intimacy and fear of being rejected.
16. Displacement	Individuals "displace" or transfer an emotion from its original object to a more acceptable substitute.	A man who is angry at his boss but afraid to be aware of his anger comes home and criticizes his wife for minor things or spanks his child for something he normally would have ignored. Another example is a five-year-old girl with unconscious conflicts about her intense love for her father, including a desire to marry him when she grows up; she displaces her love to her teddy bear and takes it everywhere she goes.
17. Dissociation	Individuals "dissociate" or detach emotional significance and effect from an idea, situation, or object.	A pastor crusades for sexual purity and integrity but is unconsciously seductive with female counselees, dissociating his guilt feelings and sexual feelings from his actions. He thus can still consider himself faultless in the situation and is not consciously hypocritical. Split personalities, fugue states, and amnesia—more severe forms of dissociation—are all considered severe histrionic personality characteristics.

Unconscious Defense Mechanisms Frequently Seen in Counseling (Cont.)

Name	Description	Example
18. Unhealthy Identification	Individuals model their values, attitudes, and behavior after another person without even knowing that they are doing so.	A child watching a violent "hero" on television, a teen-ager watching seductive behavior in movies, or an adult observing underhanded business methods of an employer are good illustrations of this defense mechanism. Individuals can also "identify" with group values and attitudes, as in cults.
19. Regression	Individuals faced with current conflicts return to an earlier stage of emotional immaturity where they felt more protected from life's stresses.	A four-year-old boy who is totally toilet trained and maturing satisfactorily suddenly has a younger brother born into his family. He has unconscious conflicts about his mother being in the hospital for a week, then spending much of her time with the baby and less with him. Without knowing why, he suddenly begins to regress to bedwetting, baby-talk, soiling his pants, temper tantrums, and hyperactivity. Unconsciously he is returning to infancy in hopes that he will again receive his mother's individual attention. This is a very common occurrence. Regression can occur in adults during times of stress such as moving, a job change, having a first child, physical illness, or death of a loved one. Most hospital patients behave less maturely than they would normally when well and at home.
20. Undoing	Individuals carry out unconscious acts or verbal communications to negate a previous mistake, as though the mistake never occurred.	On a date a young woman's declaration of love is warm but later she convinces herself that she was only joking and treats her date politely but coldly. Another example would be a Christian criticizing a fellow Christian, then feeling unconscious guilt the next day and going out of his way to compliment the person he criticized without remembering that he had been critical or knowing why he is being so complimentary. *Undoing* is not to be confused with its healthy counterpart, which is purposeful—a conscious restitution or apology for wrongs that have been done.

Unconscious Defense Mechanisms Frequently Seen in Counseling (Cont.)

Name	Description	Example
21. Somatization	Unacceptable unconscious feelings (such as anger) or motives (such as vengeance) are represented by physical symptoms (such as headaches, diarrhea or heartburn) in parts of the body inner-vated by the autonomic nervous system. Such persons are thus able to keep their minds on their physical symptoms to avoid being aware of their true feelings and motives. Most people use this defense mechanism regularly. Histrionic personalities and hypochondriacs use it excessively.	A college professor corrects one of his students in class in a less than tactful way. The student becomes angry but is afraid to be aware of his anger because he might get in trouble with the profes-sor if he lets the professor know about his anger. Since the student holds in his anger, his body responds with almost immediate tightness of lower-back mus-cles. Lactic acid accumulates and puts pressure on nerve endings in his back muscles within a few hours. Several days later he becomes immobilized by severe back pain and sees a physician. The physician will either (1) give him pain medications, (2) refer him to a psy-chiatrist, or (3) if dishonest, diagnose the problem as a "pinched nerve" and oper-ate on his back unnecessarily.
22. Unhealthy Sublimation	Consciously unacceptable drives (such as hostility or lust) are acceptably chan-neled without the individual ever be-coming aware that the unacceptable drives exist within. It would be healthier to become aware of such drives, pray about them, do something about them, and then consciously *redirect* the drives.	A boy grows up in a cold, critical, hostile, but strict religious family. Being aware of his own strong hostile drives would hurt his pride and conscience, so he becomes an expert hunter as a boy, killing many "acceptable" animals. In high school and college he becomes an exceptional middle linebacker in football, noted for his "killer instinct." He then goes to medical school and sur-gery residency, spending the rest of his life cutting people's bodies to save their lives. All of those activities help him to redirect his hostile drives so that he never becomes aware of their existence. He would angrily deny their existence if they were pointed out to him.

Unconscious Defense Mechanisms Frequently Seen in Counseling (Cont.)

Name	Description	Example
23. Hysterical (Histrionic) Conversion Reaction	Unacceptable feelings (such as anger) or motives (such as vengeance) result in actual, symbolic loss of function of a part of the body innervated by sensory or motor nerves.	A right-handed mother has a sudden urge to kill her misbehaving child but rapidly represses that unacceptable urge, becoming instantly paralyzed in her right arm. Another common example would be a histrionic female with multiple, lifelong sexual conflicts who loses all sensation in her genital area and no longer enjoys sex with her husband. During the Vietnamese war many American soldiers became paralyzed in one arm. It was noted that the paralyzed arm was nearly always the individual's primary shooting arm. Under hypnosis the soldiers could use the paralyzed arm, which again became paralyzed when not under hypnosis. Such hysterical conversion symptoms (including hysterical paralysis, blindness, deafness, multiple sclerosis symptoms, or seizures) are readily reversible with psychiatric counseling and the power of suggestion. Nearly all "faith healings" in histrionic, emotional church services are hysterical conversions that are being given up without the realization by the individual that the lost function was psychological in the first place. Such "healings" are not to be confused with genuine supernatural healings, which God carried out in Bible times to prove that Christianity was real, and may still carry out today.
24. Complex Formation	A number of related or apparently unrelated ideas in the unconscious are associated in such a way that any environmental stimulus that threatens to bring one of them into conscious awareness evokes the emotion that has been associated with the entire group.	A young girl experiences extreme anxiety while she is being jumped on and bitten by a black dog. She later represses the entire event. As an adult she doesn't understand why she develops anxiety symptoms whenever a black cat crosses her path.
25. Condensation	Individuals react to a single word, phrase, or idea with all of the emotions that they unconsciously associate with a complex group of ideas. Condensation is similar to complex formation.	An advertising agency comes up with a brief but catchy slogan that doubles the sale of an otherwise unremarkable product because the slogan arouses rewarding, unconscious emotions associated with a complex group of prior experiences in a large segment of the population.
26. Symbolization	A single act or object represents a complex group of acts or objects, some of which are unacceptable to the ego. Symbolization is similar to complex formation and condensation.	A soldier is asked by his wife why he volunteered for a dangerous assignment that would take him far away from home. He tells her he wanted "to defend the flag," but refuses to discuss her questions about the relevance of the war itself, or the need of their children to have a live, present father.

Unconscious Defense Mechanisms Frequently Seen in Counseling (Cont.)

Name	Description	Example
27. Idealization	Individuals overestimate the admired attributes of another person.	A pastor is frequently idealized by members of a congregation, resulting in great disappointment when they find out he has normal human temptations and drives.
28. Compensation	Individuals attempt to make up for real or imagined personal deficiencies in physique, performance, talents, or psychological attributes. This can become a healthy defense if the compensation is done consciously and with proper motives. Compensation here, however, refers to an unconscious striving to make up for inferiority feelings resulting from lack of acceptance of the way God made us.	A young woman decides to use lots of makeup and becomes sexually promiscuous without realizing that she is doing so to compensate for severe inferiority feelings over her (real or imagined) unattractiveness.
29. Aim Inhibition	Individuals deceive themselves about their true desires and end up accepting partial or modified fulfillment of those desires.	A young man feels a strong conviction to become a missionary but unconsciously struggles with the hardships of leaving his home country. He convinces himself that he never really wanted to become a missionary in the first place and ends up with a secular job, but heads up the missionary society of his local church (unconsciously to ease his hidden guilt feelings). Aim inhibition is sometimes called substitution.
30. Sarcasm	Individuals with repressed hostility toward themselves, another individual, or a group ventilate that hostility without even being aware of its existence by making critical jokes about themselves or the others.	A young man is not aware that he has much repressed hostility toward his mother and women in general. He makes up constant critical jokes about women being ignorant or inferior and doesn't understand why some individuals are offended by his "innocent sarcasm." Another individual who has repressed hostility toward himself for not being more successful sarcastically jokes about Blacks, Poles, or other minority groups (who unconsciously remind him of himself) to ventilate his own self-hatred unconsciously.

Unconscious Defense Mechanisms Frequently Seen in Counseling (Cont.)

Name	Description	Example
31. Magical Thinking	Individuals compensate for inferiority feelings by thinking they have subtle supernatural powers.	An immature Christian is seeking God's will on whether or not to marry the non-Christian girl he has "fallen in love" with. Rather than seeking out mature counselors and the advice of God's Word, he uses "magical thinking" by opening up the Bible at random, looking at the first verse he comes to, reads, "Go ye and do likewise," and concludes that it is definitely God's will to marry that non-Christian girl. An eight-year-old girl becomes very angry at her father and has a fleeting wish that he would die. That night she has a nightmare about her father dying. The next day her father really does die in an automobile accident. She naively believes that her anger actually caused her father's death and becomes overwhelmed with guilt and depression. Magical thinking, to a mild degree, is present in nearly all persons. It is present to a greater degree in compulsive adults and in young children of all personality types. It is present in psychotic proportions in individuals suffering from schizophrenia.
32. Incorporation	Symbolic representations of a person or parts of a person are figuratively ingested.	A young boy feels inferior to his father because his father has larger, stronger legs. The boy represses these unacceptable thoughts and feelings. Whenever his family eats fried chicken for dinner, he always wants the drumsticks. Part of his unconscious motivation is to eat chicken legs to make his own legs larger and stronger like his father's. Consciously, he thinks it is only because he likes the taste of dark meat.

Unconscious Defense Mechanisms Frequently Seen in Counseling (Cont.)

Name	Description	Example
33. Acting Out	An individual who is unaware of his unacceptable urges (such as craving the affection of a frequently absent parent of the opposite sex) acts out these urges through such behaviors as sexual promiscuity or compulsive stealing.	A teen-age girl feels totally ignored by her traveling-salesman father. She represses her craving for his love and approval, then finds herself being sexually promiscuous with boys who unconsciously remind her (in appearance or personality) of her father. She also compulsively steals things from males (uncles, male teachers) without knowing why. In reality the compulsive stealing is an unconscious, symbolic way to steal the love of her father which she misses. Thus the acting out of unmet cravings is a common defense mechanism, especially in teen-agers and in adults who become involved in sexual promiscuity and compulsive stealing. Subtle teen-age rebellion can also be an acting out of repressed anger toward parents if the teen-ager is unaware of his/her motives for breaking those rules, but the term *acting out* is usually used in the context of sexual sins or stealing. It is closely related to the defense mechanism called *sexualization*.
34. Intellectualization	Individuals avoid becoming aware of their severe inferiority feelings and other unconscious conflicts by the excessive use of intellectual vocabulary, discussions, and philosophies. This is a very common defense. It is used excessively by emotionally unstable borderline schizophrenics who relate to others only on an intellectual basis to stay in touch with reality. Becoming aware of their repressed emotions too rapidly would result in a schizophrenic break. Psychiatrists strip away this defense mechanism carefully and slowly as they build up borderline individuals in other ways.	A boy grows up in a very critical, cold, upper-class family. Because of their unconscious inferiority feelings, his parents regard with disdain anyone whose likes and dislikes are not up to their "cultural" level. The boy gets A's and B's throughout his school years but this is not good enough to satisfy his parents. His inferiority feelings worsen and he comes close to a schizophrenic break with reality. In college he becomes a philosophy major, uses lots of long, rarely used words, talks only about philosophical issues (never about his own feelings) and looks down on people who are less intellectual than himself.

Unconscious Defense Mechanisms Frequently Seen in Counseling (Cont.)

Name	Description	Example
35. Hypochondriasis	Individuals convince themselves that they are physically ill when they really aren't or else exaggerate in their own minds the severity of an illness they actually do have. Hypochondriasis is more general than the specific defense mechanisms of somatization and hysterical conversion reaction.	A man in his forties who is lazy but nevertheless working to support his family develops a legitimate lower-back problem. He is laid up for six weeks, during which time he is pampered, doesn't have to do anything responsible, and enjoys watching television all day. Because of all that "secondary gain," he unconsciously convinces himself that his back is still in terrible condition even after it has healed completely. His wife goes to work to support the family, and he is able to avoid responsibility without feeling consciously guilty and without the criticism of his wife, who believes he is still physically ill. Eventually his unconscious guilt (or boredom) gets to him, he goes to a "faith healing" service, and is miraculously healed. He has not consciously deceived anyone during the entire course of events.
36. Blocking	Individuals experience a sudden cessation of the flow of thought or speech in the middle of a sentence. When such individuals, with conscious effort, try to continue the thought, new ideas crop up which are unrelated to the original sentence.	A young woman is talking to her boyfriend and during the conversation an unconscious conflict threatens to emerge to her awareness. Her unconscious mind immediately blocks from her memory what she was about to say, she loses her train of thought, then begins to talk about an unrelated subject that is less threatening to her ego.
37. Controlling	Insecure individuals who are relatively unaware of their severe feelings of powerlessness (and inadequacy to perform up to their superegos' standards) develop strong urges to think for and control other individuals, which cause themselves to feel more powerful.	A thirty-year-old engineer with a compulsive personality almost has a nervous breakdown because of extreme insecurity and anxiety. He "falls in love" with a very dependent, histrionic female, whom he controls totally in marriage, making nearly every decision for her. He thus wards off some of his feelings of insecurity by controlling her. He may even use "biblical submission" as a rationalization for his excessive domination.
38. Compartmentalization	Individuals unconsciously experience their attitudes as though they were unconnected and unrelated—in separate compartments of their brains—to hide from their conscious awareness the conflicts between their real unacceptable feelings and motives and their idealized feelings and motives.	A severely anxious adult male starts to become aware of unconscious guilt feelings when he starts to see the relationship between his current fantasy and a recent conflict he had. His unconscious immediately convinces him that the fantasy and conflict are unrelated, so he feels at ease temporarily and starts thinking about something else.

Unconscious Defense Mechanisms Frequently Seen in Counseling (Cont.)		
Name	Description	Example
39. Externalization	Individuals with a weak ego experience their inner thought processes and feelings as though they were occurring outside the self. They go through life experiencing themselves in and through others vicariously. Their idealized self is also externalized so that their identity becomes intwined with another individual of the same sex who is perceived temporarily as their "ideal" companion. This often leads to homosexual behavior or severe inferiority feelings.	A male borderline schizophrenic holds on to reality by externalizing nearly all of his conflicts and attributes. He develops a crush on another male whom he perceives as the type of person he would like to be himself. They have a homosexual affair that lasts until he realizes that his ego-ideal lover is not at all what he expected him to be.
40. Sexualization	Individuals deceive themselves about their inferiority feelings or hostility toward the opposite sex by focusing on their own sexual prowess. They may do that through actual sexual encounter with another person or through sexual fantasy. In either case, "conquering" the opposite sex enables them temporarily to feel less inferior sexually and also serves as a means to ventilate hostility toward the opposite sex.	A twenty-one-year-old female was sexually abused by her father at age thirteen. He otherwise ignored her most of her life. She has deep-seated and intense repressed hostility toward him even though she thinks she has forgiven him. At age twenty-one she becomes very promiscuous to conquer males and use them to feed her ego. She doesn't care if they are already married because if their lives were ruined it would be unconsciously satisfying to her. She is unaware of her hostility toward men, consciously claiming that she loves men. 1 John 2:16 lists lust of the flesh (sexualization) along with lust of the eyes (materialism) and the pride of life (control, power, prestige) as the three primary ways in which human beings compensate for their inner conflicts.

sinning—but *never* to have a grudge-holding, vengeful spirit (Eph. 4:26; Lev. 19:17–18).

2. *Confession.* The primary conscious defense against the emotional pain that comes from true guilt is confession of sins to God (agreeing with God that the sin committed was wrong), followed by an attitude of forgiveness toward self (1 John 1:9). Christians are encouraged to confess their sins to each other and are promised that such confession will result in physical/ spiritual healing (James 5:16).

3. *Patience.* Patience is an excellent conscious defense against the frequent minor frustrations of life. Selfish, immature individuals who give themselves too many rights are constantly plagued with anger, since so many of their "rights" are violated. Giving up those rights to God and expecting fewer things to be

perfect will result in patience, greater humility, less anger, and greater joy in life.

4. *Love.* Love is a conscious choice. A mature person loves another person because he or she chooses to love that other person and to behave lovingly toward the person. The feeling of love follows the action, which follows the conscious choice. The giving and accepting of genuine Christian love is the primary conscious defense against inferiority feelings and loneliness. The Great Commandment given by Christ in Luke 10:25–27 includes loving God, others, and self (an expression of godly self-worth).

5. *Faith.* Anxiety, basically, is lack of faith. An individual who does not have faith in what that individual and God can do together as a team will be troubled with anxiety, possibly even with insomnia. Faith is thus the primary conscious spiritual and psychological defense against anxiety. Solomon encouraged God's children to have faith in God's principles ("sound wisdom and discretion"). "Then you will go on your way in safety, and your foot will not stumble; when you lie down, you will not be afraid; when you lie down, your sleep will be sweet" (Prov. 3:23–24; see also 3:5–7).

6. *Healthy Compensation.* Individuals aware of personal deficiencies (correctable defects) can obtain God's help to overcome such deficiencies (Phil. 4:13). That not only increases our self-worth but also makes us more efficient tools that can be used for furthering the cause of Christ.

7. *Altruism.* Altruism is basically doing good deeds to please the Lord and has the following benefits: (a) It furthers the cause of Christ and is an act of obedience to God. (b) It increases the altruistic person's self-worth (it is easier for us to like ourselves when we are worthwhile to others). (c) It enables altruistic persons to get their minds off themselves and worry less about minor personal frustrations. (d) It builds friendships, which are essential for mental health.

8. *Anticipation.* Anticipating a future difficult situation with a prayerful, trusting attitude can reduce anxiety. A good example is Jesus Christ facing His terrible death on the cross. In spite of His prayerful anticipation in the garden, Christ still suffered so much anxiety and grief that "his sweat was like drops of blood" (Luke 22:44). Nevertheless, He used anticipation to prepare

Himself to bear temporary separation from the Father while enduring a painful death on the cross for our sins.

9. *Conscious Control.*   Most individuals are too passive. They go through life passively allowing conflicts to rise and passively waiting for their conflicts to "go away." Yet very few conflicts go away by merely waiting them out. Taking conscious control means becoming responsible and making conscious choices for overcoming conflicts. Conscious control enables individuals to overcome many of the unconscious defense mechanisms which would control their behavior if they remained passive.

10. *Healthy Identification.*   Healthy identification means making conscious choices to develop some godly personality characteristics seen in other Christians we admire. God doesn't expect any Christian to try to become someone else, but the apostle Paul encouraged his converts to mimic some of his own godly behavior. A Christian's primary identification, however, should be with Jesus Christ (Rom. 8:29).

11. *Humor.*   One of the fruits of the Spirit is joy. The ability to have fun and enjoy life and the ability to laugh at oneself are definite signs of mental and spiritual health. Laughing at our own minor mistakes that we make daily (like being forgetful) is much better than self-condemnation for not being perfect.

12. *Redirection.*   Redirection is the conscious, healthy counterpart of the unconscious defense mechanism of sublimation. The difference is that with redirection mature individuals can become aware of some unwanted psychological or spiritual conflict (such as repressed hostility) and consciously dissipate some of their hostile energy while they are in the process of getting rid of repressed hostility through prayer, forgiveness, and other means.

13. *Restitution.*   When mature individuals offend someone, they show genuine humility and concern for the offended individual by making restitution. Restitution can be a verbal apology, or it may require financial payment for damages done to someone else's possessions.

14. *Healthy Suppression.*   Suppressing the truth without first dealing with the problem is a sin. Obsession over a past failure without forgiving oneself is equally sinful, however.

Mature individuals confess past errors to God, forgive themselves, and then suppress the past errors so they can concentrate
on present or future concerns. Nor should we rest on past suc-
cesses, with no motivation to accomplish future goals for God.
The apostle Paul stated, "Forgetting what is behind and straining
toward what is ahead, I press on toward the goal to win the prize
for which God has called me heavenward in Christ Jesus" (Phil.
3:13–14).

   15. *Dreaming.*   Adults usually dream twenty minutes out of
every ninety that they are asleep, a conclusion determined from
EEG patterns. Most people do not realize that they dream so
much because they never remember their dreams unless they
wake up during one. Dreams are mediated biochemically by
serotonin and norepinephrine, the same brain amines that when
depleted result in clinical depression. Holding grudges, for example, depletes these essential brain amines. Many research
studies have shown that normal, mature individuals, when
deprived of dream time (even though they get enough nondream
sleep), begin to develop depressive or even psychotic symptoms
within three nights of dream deprivation. God somehow uses
dreams each night to help us resolve unconscious conflicts, or at
least to dissipate some of the emotional pain tied to unconscious
conflicts. A normal, spiritual, unmarried adult male, for example,
will be relieved of his biological sexual tensions by having "wet
dreams," perhaps several times a week. Newborn babies, facing
the real world outside of the mother's womb for the first time,
may spend ten hours dreaming each day. Christians should not
deprive themselves of sleep. Sleeping and dreaming are gifts of
God to maintain our sanity.

5

The Christian
Eclectic Approach

It has been estimated that more than 250 methods of psychotherapy are in use today. How is the novice counselor to know which one is best? From our experience as Christian psychiatrists we have come to the conclusion that the wisest policy is to follow what we have chosen to designate the "Christian eclectic approach." Central to this approach is our conviction that the Bible must be the foundation of every therapeutic effort. The Bible is divine revelation. No scientific knowledge can produce results equal to those produced by the Word of God.

On the other hand, natural revelation (scientific data) can be helpful (consider the discovery of penicillin in the 1920s). With this in mind one may legitimately draw from the methodologies of various schools. It would be naive to think that one school has discovered most of the truth while the others have little. Many schools possess a measure of the truth, but none has all of it. Therefore, it is necessary to be selective. It would be foolish to expect all counselees to respond to one therapeutic method. Rather, the counselor should have a variety of methods at his disposal and use the one that will best help his client. In other words, it is the counselor, not the counselee, who should adapt. In choosing the most appropriate method or combination of methods given the particular situation (the eclectic approach), the wise counselor will always be mindful that the only absolute standard is the Word of God.

With the proliferation of various schools of thought, it will be helpful to place them in several broad categories. This grouping will offer some sense of order to the Christian counselor groping amid the confusing complexity of methods available today. Of all the attempts to categorize the various schools of psychotherapy, that of Toksoz Karaus is most useful for our purposes.[1] We will summarize his classification of schools into three basic divisions: insight-oriented, behavior-oriented, and experiential-oriented. We will then touch briefly on a fourth (the biochemical-oriented) and add our own (the Christian eclectic approach).

Insight-oriented Schools

The insight-oriented schools teach that mental problems develop because of unconscious, unresolved conflicts from childhood. Mental health results as one begins to gain in-depth insight into how these unconscious conflicts affect him today. The ultimate goal is to help the counselee resolve these conflicts. An example of the insight-oriented schools is psychoanalysis (including all its short-term variations). (See Figure 7 for lists of representative techniques used by the insight-oriented schools and by the other major schools of secular psychotherapy.)

Behavior-oriented Schools

The behavior-oriented schools teach that mental problems manifest themselves in inappropriate behavior. This inappropriate behavior may have been learned or conditioned at an early age; it may involve overt fears or faulty beliefs. In any event, it is the view of the behavior-oriented schools that new behavior can be learned. Desensitization techniques are used in behavior modification; new beliefs are instilled by cognitive therapy; more-responsible behavior is taught in reality therapy.

Experiential-oriented Schools

In general, the experiential-oriented schools focus on feelings. Their techniques often revolve around getting the client in touch with his true feelings or arousing negative feelings. Examples of

1. Toksoz B. Karaus, "Psychotherapies: An Overview," *American Journal of Psychiatry* 134.8 (1977): 851–63.

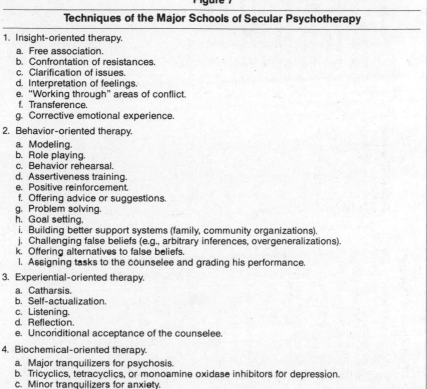

Figure 7

Techniques of the Major Schools of Secular Psychotherapy

1. Insight-oriented therapy.
   a. Free association.
   b. Confrontation of resistances.
   c. Clarification of issues.
   d. Interpretation of feelings.
   e. "Working through" areas of conflict.
   f. Transference.
   g. Corrective emotional experience.

2. Behavior-oriented therapy.
   a. Modeling.
   b. Role playing.
   c. Behavior rehearsal.
   d. Assertiveness training.
   e. Positive reinforcement.
   f. Offering advice or suggestions.
   g. Problem solving.
   h. Goal setting.
   i. Building better support systems (family, community organizations).
   j. Challenging false beliefs (e.g., arbitrary inferences, overgeneralizations).
   k. Offering alternatives to false beliefs.
   l. Assigning tasks to the counselee and grading his performance.

3. Experiential-oriented therapy.
   a. Catharsis.
   b. Self-actualization.
   c. Listening.
   d. Reflection.
   e. Unconditional acceptance of the counselee.

4. Biochemical-oriented therapy.
   a. Major tranquilizers for psychosis.
   b. Tricyclics, tetracyclics, or monoamine oxidase inhibitors for depression.
   c. Minor tranquilizers for anxiety.
   d. Lithium for manic symptoms.

experiential-oriented schools include the Rogerian school, the gestalt school, and primal-scream therapy.

The wise counselor draws from each of the three groups we have briefly characterized. In some instances one of these approaches is obviously the best course to follow. But it is often advisable to make use of all of them. Take, for example, the particular program we adopted in treating a young woman who came to our office for counseling. (1) She was helped to gain *insight* into the unresolved conflicts she had with her father and into the negative effects these conflicts had on her relationship with her husband. (2) She was also helped to deal with bitter

Figure 8

Four Types of Therapy*

	Insight-oriented	Behavior-oriented	Experiential-oriented	Christian
Representative Schools	1. Psychoanalysis (Freud) 2. Analytical psychology (Jung) 3. Individual psychology (Adler) 4. Psychoanalytic psychotherapy (Fromm, Reichmann) 5. Short-term psychotherapy (Sifneos, Malan) 6. Hypnoanalysis (Wolberg) 7. Brief or emergency psychotherapy	1. Reciprocal inhibition or behavior therapy (Wolpe) 2. Modeling therapy (Bandura) 3. Directive psychology (Thorne) 4. Behavior modification (for use with inpatients) 5. Rational-emotive therapy (Ellis) 6. Reality therapy (Glasser) 7. Transactional analysis (Berne) 8. Biofeedback (Green)	1. Client-centered (Rogers) 2. Gestalt (Perls) 3. Primal scream (Janov) 4. Logotherapy (Frankel) 5. Reparenting	1. Psychology more important than Scripture 2. Psychology parallel with Scripture 3. Scripture opposed to psychology 4. Scripture integrated with psychology 5. Scripture integrated with but regarded as more important than psychology
Basic Divisions	A continuum from short-term to psychoanalysis	1. Earlier schools—emphasis on overt fears and behavior 2. More recent schools—emphasis on beliefs (Ellis) 3. Majority of most-recent schools—emphasis on biofeedback	1. Philosophic (Rogers) 2. Somatic	See above
Mental Disorders Treated	Neuroses, personality disorders	Some neuroses, psychoses	Low self-image	All
Concept of Pathology	Unconscious conflicts	Inappropriate learned behavior	Loss of human potential	Physical, psychological, and spiritual difficulties (holistic view)
Goal of Treatment	Conflict resolution	Removal of inappropriate behavior	Actualization of potential	Health of the whole man, especially spiritual maturity

	Mode of Attaining Goal			
	In-depth insight	Direct learning	Immediate experiencing	Eclectic approach—depending on needs of the individual
Time Focus	Past	Objective present	The moment	Past-present-future
Type of Treatment	Long-term, intense	Short-term, not intense	Short-term, intense	Length and intensity vary
Counselor's Task	To comprehend unconscious	To shape behavior	To express himself openly	To understand and treat the problems of the whole man
Counselor's Role	Indirect—to reflect and interrupt	Direct and practical—to advise	To accept the counselee without condition	To determine and utilize an approach suitable to the particular situation (see 1 Thess. 5:14)
Techniques	Free association, transference	Conditioning	A variety including verbal and somatic methods	Use of Scripture and scientific methods
Treatment Model	Doctor–patient (therapeutic alliance)	Teacher–student (learning alliance)	Peer–peer (human alliance)	Shepherd–member of flock (spiritual alliance)
Nature of Relationship	Artificial relationship for the purpose of finding a cure	Genuine, but for the sake of finding a cure	Genuine, but primarily to find a cure	Genuine relationship which is used in the search for a cure
Crucial Point Ignored by the General Theory	Insight alone may not result in change	Man is more than a computer	Man is not all good	

*Most of this figure is based on Toksoz B. Karaus, "Psychotherapies: An Overview," *American Journal of Psychiatry* 134.8 (1977): 851–63. Used by permission of the American Psychiatric Association. The characterization of Christian counseling is based in part on John D. Carter, "Secular and Sacred Models of Psychology and Religion," *Journal of Psychology and Theology* (1977): 197–208, and in part on our own ideas and experience.

feelings which had been there all along, but had been repressed
and manifested themselves in passive-aggressive behavior. (3) She
was encouraged to make appropriate changes in her daily
behavior in order to improve relationships with her husband
and friends.

Biochemical-oriented Schools

We must also make mention of the biochemical-oriented
schools, which have many followers and may in fact be the major
force in psychiatry today. The proponents of these schools teach
that mental problems are the results of biochemical, physiological, and neurological abnormalities. In their view mental
problems can be resolved by correcting these biochemical
abnormalities.

The Christian Eclectic Approach

Finally we consider the category of "Christian counseling."[2]
There are various subdivisions within this category: (1) those
schools which place greater emphasis on psychology than on
Scripture; (2) those schools which feel that Scripture and psychology parallel each other but never meet; (3) those schools
which feel that Scripture is opposed to psychology; and (4) those
schools which integrate the two. We place ourselves firmly within
the last subdivision. Of course, even here it must be stressed that
Scripture is divine revelation and can produce supernatural
results. Psychology in and of itself can never do what Scripture
can. Psychology can be extremely helpful. One can learn much
from it. But formal psychological theory and Scripture are not
on the same plane. (See Figure 8 for a comparison of the Christian approach with the insight-oriented, behavior-oriented, and
experiential-oriented schools.)

Now that we have briefly looked at the four major groups of
secular psychotherapy and those schools which are categorized
as "Christian counseling," it is time to restate our approach. We

2. See John D. Carter, "Secular and Sacred Models of Psychology and
Religion," *Journal of Psychology and Theology* (1977): 197–208.

incorporate in our counseling the methods employed by all four major groups mentioned previously. We-examine each case on an individual basis and carefully determine which of the methods will be of greatest use. We take the best from each of the major categories of psychotherapy. We employ, then, an eclectic approach. But underlying all our decisions in these matters is a burning concern to insure that the Bible is central to our counseling techniques. Not only is the Word of God to be used in conjunction with the therapies of the secular schools, it is to be the overriding factor. Thus it is that we choose to label our counseling method the "Christian eclectic approach."

6

An Analysis
of Several Key Topics

In this chapter we will focus on several key topics: counsel(ing), anxiety, guilt, anger, and a balanced approach involving behavior, feelings, and belief systems. Each topic will be examined under three headings: (1) definition, (2) biblical correlations and integrations, and (3) methodology. We will concentrate on spiritual and psychological aspects. Of course, as we have noted in earlier chapters, spiritual and psychological aspects can have ramifications involving the physical. For example, David said:

> When I kept silent about my sin, my body wasted away
> Through my groaning all day long.
> For day and night Thy hand was heavy upon me;
> My vitality was drained away as with the fever-heat of summer.
> I acknowledged my sin to Thee,
> And my iniquity I did not hide;
> I said, "I will confess my transgressions to the Lord";
> And Thou didst forgive the guilt of my sin (Ps. 32:3–5, NASB).

Also, the wise Solomon said:

> My son, give attention to my words;
> Incline your ear to my sayings.
> Do not let them depart from your sight;
> Keep them in the midst of your heart.
> For they are life to those that find them,
> And health to all their whole body (Prov. 4:20–22, NASB).

Counsel(ing)

Definition

In general the word *counsel* refers to advice given as a result of consultation. Although different schools of psychological thought vary greatly in their methodology, the actual intent of counseling is nearly always the same, namely, to assist someone (who has asked for help) in dealing with a problem.

Biblical Correlations and Integrations

In the New Testament there are a number of Greek words pertaining to counsel. Five of them can be found in 1 Thessalonians 5:14 alone:

1. *Parakaleō*—to beseech, exhort, encourage, comfort (Rom. 12:1; 15:30; 2 Cor. 1:4).
2. *Noutheteō*—to put in mind, warn, confront (Rom. 15:14; 1 Cor. 4:14; Col. 3:16).
3. *Paramutheomai*—to cheer up, encourage (1 Thess. 2:11).
4. *Antechomai*—to cling to, to hold fast to, to take an interest in.
5. *Makrothumeō*—to be patient (Matt. 18:26, 29; Heb. 6:15; James 5:7).

Moreover, in the Old Testament there are several Hebrew words pertaining to counsel:

1. *dābār*—the "counsel of Balaam" (Num. 31:16) refers to advice.
2. *yā'ats*—"Then the prophet stopped and said, 'I know that God has planned to destroy you, because you have done this, and have not listened to my counsel'" (2 Chron. 25:16, NASB). Here again counsel pertains to advice and direction.
3. *sōwd*—David's reference to the "sweet counsel" (Ps. 55:14, KJV) he had received from a former friend carries the connotation of fellowship and sharing.

4. *'ēṭā'*—that Daniel answered Arioch "with counsel" (Dan. 2:14, KJV) implies that he responded with discretion.
5. *'ētsāh*—Israel's lack "in counsel" (Deut. 32:28) suggests a lack of understanding.
6. *yāsad*—"the rulers take counsel together" (Ps. 2:2) means that they sit down together for a period of mutual consultation, deliberation, and instruction.

That the Bible uses several words for counsel seems to imply that different approaches are suitable for different situations, a view substantiated by the findings of modern psychology.

Methodology: Ways to Counsel

1. *Listening.* By simply listening the counselor can help the counselee to unburden himself of deep-seated hurts and to begin to feel understood. Elihu (Job 32) was a good listener.
2. *Self-disclosure.* The counselor may wish to share personal examples from his own life (if they will help rather than hinder the counselee). The apostle Paul used this technique.
3. *Directives.* Straightforward, direct advice is often beneficial. Christ frequently used this approach as did Solomon.
4. *Indirect Techniques.* Stories, parables, and questions can be used to help a person gain insight. Christ often taught others by asking them questions or telling parables. In the Old Testament Nathan used a story to help David discern his own sin.
5. *Combination of Directives and Indirect Techniques.* In our practice we often begin by using indirect techniques to help the counselee gain insight into himself; then we give direct advice based on the Bible as absolute standard.

Anxiety

Definition

Anxiety is a painful or apprehensive uneasiness of mind usually over an impending or anticipated ill. There are often behavioral, psychological, and physiological manifestations.

Biblical Correlations and Integrations

Scripture indicates that some anxiety (a realistic concern as seen in such verses as 1 Cor. 12:25; 2 Cor. 11:28; and Phil. 2:20) is healthy. However, intense anxiety (fretting and worrying, as seen in such verses as Luke 8:14; Phil. 4:6; and 1 Peter 5:7) is not healthy. A Greek word which is often translated "anxiety" is used about twenty-five times in the New Testament. It is usually used in the negative sense (implying worrying or fretting), but occasionally in the positive sense (a realistic concern).

Both modern psychology and Scripture point out that anxiety exists in normal and abnormal amounts. Psychologists have long noted that individuals are more efficient and productive when they have a measure of anxiety. However, if the anxiety becomes intense, one's efficiency begins to decrease accordingly.

Methodology: Suggestions to Make
to a Counselee Experiencing Anxiety

1. Determine to obey God. God commands us not to be anxious (Phil. 4:6).
2. Pray (Phil. 4:6). God told Daniel not to fear because God had heard his prayer from the time he first started praying and *He would answer* (Dan. 10:12).
3. Realize that God can keep our minds safe as we obey Him (Phil. 4:7).
4. Meditate on positive thoughts (Phil. 4:8). We have often encouraged people who catch themselves worrying to say, "Stop, relax; anxiety is a signal to relax, so relax." We then encourage them to go over and over a verse like Philippians 4:8. Anxiety is usually a signal to become more anxious, but by a simple technique of behavior modification the brain can be conditioned to use anxiety as a signal to relax. There is no better place to find positive things to meditate on than the Scriptures (Ps. 34:4; 86:15; Prov. 1:33; 3:25–26; Isa. 40:28–31; Matt. 6:33–34; 11:28–29; John 10:27–28; 14:27; Heb. 4:15; 1 John 3:20; 4:10).
5. Realize there is a twofold responsibility (yours and Christ's) in doing anything. "I can do all things through Christ . . ." (Phil. 4:13, KJV). An individual can overcome anxiety through Christ.
6. Realize that the grace of God is with you (2 Cor. 9:8; Phil.

4:23). The knowledge that one is never alone and that His grace is always present can markedly decrease anxiety.

7. Cultivate the art of living one day at a time (Matt. 6:34). Probably 98 percent of the things we are anxious or worry about never come true.[1]

Guilt

Definition

Guilt is the fact of having committed an offense or having done wrong.

Biblical Correlations and Integrations

When one thinks of guilt, one almost automatically thinks of conscience as well.[2] The functions of the conscience are ascribed to the "heart," which is a broad term used in connection with many aspects of intellectual, emotional, and moral life. Although the term *conscience* does not appear in the Old Testament, it does occur thirty-two times in the New Testament in the form of the Greek word *suneidēsis,* which literally means "to know together with."

The New Testament makes use of three Greek words which can be translated "(to be) guilty": *hupodikos, opheilō,* and *enochos.* They are generally employed in a legal sense. Theological guilt is the realization that God's divine principles have been violated. This guilt is a normal and healthy reaction in keeping with the teaching of Scripture. It is important to note that theological guilt never involves a feeling of being rejected by God because of the offense, for God never rejects His children.

To feel guilty for having offended God's principles is healthy. But can the conscience always be used as a guide in such matters? Consider the implication of a verse like Hebrews 9:14: "the blood of Christ [will] ... cleanse your conscience from dead

1. For a more extensive discussion of anxiety see Frank B. Minirth and Paul D. Meier, *Happiness Is a Choice* (Grand Rapids: Baker, 1978), pp. 167–72.

2. See John D. Carter, "Towards a Biblical Model of Counseling," *Journal of Psychology and Theology* (1980): 45–52.

works to serve the living God" (NASB). In this instance God stands
against the conscience. The key question in determining whether
the conscience is a reliable guide is, Does the conscience agree
with the Word of God? When God convicts the conscience, He
never goes against His Word.

In general, if there are no principles in the Word of God
which relate to the matter in question, feelings of guilt are
unnecessary. If such feelings do exist, the conscience may be
overly strict. Guilt which drives a person to work all the time,
and thus to pay little attention to his family and neglect daily
devotions, is unnecessary. There is no text in Scripture which
encourages guilt if one does not work all the time. In fact, the
principles of Scripture in this case would encourage less work in
order that more time might be spent with God and the family.

The guilt we feel regarding matters not explicitly covered by
scriptural principles is sometimes popularly referred to as "false
guilt." Of course, it is debatable whether guilt is ever really false
since it does in fact exist. Perhaps a more accurate term is
"unnecessary guilt," although it too has its drawbacks.

Precisely what is involved in false or unnecessary guilt? There
are several factors which complicate the issue. For example,
there is what Francis Schaeffer calls the "false tyranny of the
conscience."[3] That is, a person may continue to feel guilty even
after confessing a known sin. But with confession God forgives
and guilt should be gone. There is also the matter of actions
which are not wrong in themselves, but which offend the overly
strict conscience of weaker brothers. If a weaker brother com-
mits such an act, he sins. Paul says regarding the eating of meat
offered to idols (which does not in itself violate any of God's
principles), "He who doubts is condemned if he eats, because his
eating is not from faith; and whatever is not from faith is sin"
(Rom. 14:23, NASB).

The issue is indeed complicated. For the purpose of this discussion "false guilt" can be regarded as any guilt that is unnecessary in the sense that no specific principle in the Word of
God has been violated.[4] This in no way gives man license to do

3. Francis A. Schaeffer, *True Spirituality* (Wheaton, IL: Tyndale, 1971), p. 130.
4. For a more extensive discussion of false guilt see Frank B. Minirth et al.,
The Workaholic and His Family: An Inside Look (Grand Rapids: Baker, 1981),
pp. 111–24.

whatever he wishes. Just as many things are clearly encouraged in Scripture and should be done (e.g., letting the Word of God nourish us—1 Peter 2:2), other things are forbidden and should not be done (e.g., provoking our children to wrath—Col. 3:21). Naturally, God will convict us when we go against His Word or fail to live by it. Doing what He has forbidden will produce a healthy feeling of guilt.

Finally, what is true guilt? True guilt is the conviction of wrongdoing when we have behaved in a manner that according to Scripture is clearly illegal (e.g., overt moral sins—Gal. 5:19–21). This includes any behavior that offends a weaker brother (1 Cor. 8, etc.). Such behavior will produce a conviction of guilt. The knowledge that God loves and accepts us, but that we have offended Him, is healthy in this case.

Methodology: Suggestions to Make to a Counselee Experiencing Guilt

1. Confess true guilt (1 John 1:9) in order to restore fellowship with God and relieve any physical symptoms which may have been caused by the guilt (Ps. 32:3–5).

2. Deal with false and unnecessary guilt by being reeducated according to the Word of God. This guilt may have arisen from rigid rules in childhood that prevented development of a proper understanding of God's grace. It is essential to realize that man is unconditionally accepted (no performance necessary) by God once he trusts Christ. The heavenly Father will never reject him. Man must recognize that he is of great worth to God and has the ability to do whatever God wants him to do.

Anger

Definition

Anger is an emotional reaction of extreme displeasure. It often involves antagonism. Related terms include ire, rage, fury, indignation, and wrath.

Biblical Correlations and Integrations

That anger is a far too common emotion is suggested by the fact that the term (including its cognates) occurs 275 times in the King James translation. It is also instructive to note how many times related terms (and their cognates) appear:

abhor—43	grudge—5	strive—32
alienate—8	hate—207	variance—2
bitter—68	indignation—41	vengeance—44
despise—116	loathe—7	vex—52
enemy—375	malice—9	war—259
enmity—8	rage—25	wrath—200
fight—114	scorn—43	wroth—49
fury—70	strife—43	

Add to this the many scriptural examples of anger being carried out to the ultimate degree: Cain slew his brother Abel, Moses killed an Egyptian slavemaster, Samson slaughtered a thousand Philistines, Christ was crucified.

In studying the emotion of anger, psychology concentrates on why man becomes angry and what he can do about it. By contrast theology emphasizes man's very nature, which gives rise to his anger. The source of anger is man's old nature (he is ego-centered—see Gen. 4:5–8; 27:42–45; 49:5–7; 1 Sam. 20:30; 1 Kings 21:4; 2 Kings 5:11; Matt. 2:16; Luke 4:28). But in addition to this negative, destructive emotion, there is also a righteous anger (Exod. 11:8; Lev. 10:16–17; Neh. 5:6–13; Ps. 97:10; Mark 3:5). It should be pointed out, then, that anger does not necessarily involve sin (Eph. 4:26). On the other hand, it is often a precursor of sin or a result of sin. Perhaps more important than the source is the manner in which anger is handled.

Methodology: Suggestions to Make
to a Counselee Experiencing Anger

1. Recognize the anger; be honest about its presence.
2. Verbalize the anger to God, a friend, a counselor.
3. Determine what figures in your past (parents, spouse, self, or others) are the real targets of your anger and choose to forgive them.
4. Grow in Christ. The fruits of the Spirit (love, joy, peace, long-suffering, etc.) will work toward relieving present anger and preventing future anger.

5. Decide not to let the anger escalate. Anger does involve a choice (Prov. 14:29; 16:32; 19:11).[5]

A Balanced Approach Involving Behavior, Feelings, and Belief Systems

Definition

Behavior is the manner in which one conducts oneself. Feelings are emotional states or reactions. A belief system is the core of convictions on which one builds his life. In general, schools of psychology tend to emphasize either behavior (reality therapy, behavior modification) or feelings (psychoanalysis, the Rogerian school).

Biblical Correlations and Integrations

There are many passages in Scripture which refer specifically to proper behavior and action (Matt. 7:24; Phil. 2:13; 4:13; James 1:23–25). This fact may leave the impression that feelings are largely ignored. They are not. Christ Himself experienced and expressed deep emotions. He sighed deeply (Mark 7:34; 8:12), cried out with a loud voice (Matt. 27:46), wept (Luke 19:41; John 11:35), looked around with anger at the Pharisees (Mark 3:5), was indignant (Mark 10:14), spoke words of rebuke (Mark 8:33), and rejoiced greatly (Luke 10:21). Certainly Christ had strong feelings, was aware of these feelings, and dealt with them in appropriate ways.

It is clear, then, that Scripture lays emphasis on both behavior and feelings. It follows that biblical counseling will strive for a balanced approach emphasizing both behavior and feelings.

In recent times some schools of thought (e.g., rational-emotive therapy) have placed greater stress on belief systems than on behavior or feelings. Certainly, having our belief systems changed so that we reflect the image of Christ more clearly (Rom. 12:2) is what much of Christianity is all about. The biblical counselor will realize that the three elements (behavior, feelings, and belief systems) are closely intertwined and that he must be

5. For a more extensive discussion of ways to handle anger see Minirth and Meier, *Happiness*, pp. 149–60.

sensitive to and able to deal with all of them (as appropriate in the particular situation).

Methodology: Ways to Deal with Behavior, Feelings, and Belief Systems

1. Encourage the counselee to express his feelings. Deep-seated guilt, grief, or anger is a heavy burden to carry. Such feelings must be brought into the open so that healing can take place. Past sins may need to be confessed (1 John 1:9).

2. Help the counselee figure out specific behavior patterns he can adopt in order to begin dealing with his problem(s). An integral part of the plan for each counselee is a regular quality time with the Lord and His Word so that his belief system can change in a healthy direction.

7

Skills
of the Christian Counselor

There is a variety of skills which the Christian counselor must develop if he is to be of service to his clients. These abilities are essential throughout the counseling process—from the initial interview through final resolution of the problem. In this chapter we will touch on a number of these skills. The counselor should periodically evaluate how he measures up in each of these areas. It is often beneficial to have a colleague join in this evaluation.

The Ability to Obtain Data

If the counselor is to be successful, he must be able to obtain enough data to make judgments concerning both the nature of the problem and suitable treatment. Central to this is keen observation of any symptoms the client may manifest. In addition to general appearance, any abnormalities such as disorientation, delusions, hallucinations, obsessions, phobias, or thought disturbances are to be noted. The counselor will try to get a sense of the client's moods and interpersonal relationships.

To get a correct perspective of the client, it is essential to develop the art of asking the right question. This includes knowing how to raise and deal with the results of provocative, anxiety-arousing questions, as well as how to move from general to specific questions. The counselor must also develop the art of logically and discreetly steering the interview into difficult and painful areas (previous psychiatric problems, drug or alcohol abuse, suicide attempts). In addition, it is important to be able to explain terms clearly (e.g., "depression"), to follow up leads, and to end the interview tactfully.

The Ability to Formulate an Approach

Choosing from among the great variety of approaches and plans of action which can be adopted with respect to any individual client is one of the most difficult tasks confronted by the counselor. How is the novice counselor to know how to proceed? Our advice is for him to utilize a few basic techniques as he gets started. He will learn to vary his approach to meet the particular needs of his counselees as his experience, knowledge, and sensitivity increase. He must be patient with himself as he tries to master the complex world of counseling with its many dimensions. He will with time learn when to provide insight and when to offer support, when to stress behavior and when to focus on feelings, when to be direct and when to be indirect, when to delve into the past and when to concentrate on the present. He will also learn the importance of being himself—the counselee will have confidence in him only if he is spontaneous and nondefensive.

The difficulty of knowing how to select the right approach is underscored by the great number of options available. We can present here only a very brief general list of what the counselor can do:

1. *Offer support.* Supportive counseling is emotional and spiritual backing. Among the techniques falling under this general heading are advice (Prov. 19:20), comfort (2 Cor. 1:3-4), encouragement (Rom. 1:11-12), listening (Elihu in Job 32), and education (the letters of Paul). Supportive counseling is, of course, not limited to private sessions. The whole body of Christ has great potential as a source of support for individuals in need of help.

2. *Provide insight.* The parables of Christ enlightened His audiences to truths about themselves which they would not otherwise have perceived. Nathan the prophet used a similar approach to make David aware of his sin.

3. *Urge confession* (James 5:16).

4. *Give positive verbal reinforcement* (Rom. 1:8).

5. *Present a Christian example.* Many biblical personalities

modeled godly conduct to others. Recall Moses' example to Joshua, Naomi's example to Ruth, Christ's example to His disciples.

6. *Educate the counselee;* that is, challenge his false beliefs (Gal. 4:9). The Christian counselor can offer God's truths in their stead. A most useful procedure in this case is to give the client homework assignments.

7. *Work with the client in a group setting.* Scripture frequently stresses the importance and personal benefits of interaction with others—love one another, bear one another's burdens, be ye kind to one another (1 Cor. 12; Eph. 4:14–16).

8. *Begin a counseling program with the client's family.* There is a strong emphasis on the family in both the Old and New Testaments. The apostle Paul gave much advice on family life (Eph. 5:22–33; 6:1–4).

9. *Utilize modern techniques for improving behavior.* Among the techniques available are assertiveness training, behavior rehearsal, and positive and negative reinforcement.

We have up to this point touched only the surface. Among other plans of action which the counselor can adopt are mediated catharsis, admonishment (1 Thess. 5:14), confrontation, and urging the counselee to reflection or self-disclosure.

In many instances the counselor will find that one method of approach is insufficient. Support alone may not be enough. Insight alone may not be enough (Solomon had much insight but still fell into sin). Likewise, listening or catharsis alone may have little impact on the counselee's life. There need to be specific behavioral changes. Scripture repeatedly emphasizes the importance of proper Christian activity (Matt. 7:24; Phil. 2:13; 4:13). If there is little or no change for the better in the client's behavior within a reasonable time, some additional approach(es) should be adopted. In such cases we have often found it helpful for the counselee to examine his own plan for life (i.e., to take a close look at the way he is actually living). Then we assist him to make appropriate changes. We call this going from plan A to plan B. Plan B recommends specific daily activities that will produce health. Among the recommendations are social interactions, exercise, recreation, and a quiet time. This plan needs to be explicit and should be reevaluated periodically.

If all of this should prove inadequate, the counselor will recognize that additional factors may be involved and that further evaluation is necessary. There may be a need for specialized psychological tests. Or referral of the counselee for an extensive physical exam, psychiatric medication, or hospitalization may be called for.

Modeling Christlike Attitudes

It is essential that the Christian counselor make a conscious effort to be like Christ. The more closely the counselor patterns his manner of dealing with clients after the manner in which Jesus dealt with the people of His time, the more successful he will be. One of the most striking features of Jesus' ministry is the variety of attitudes He displayed. At times He was gentle and passive. On other occasions He was active and friendly, or kind but firm. If the circumstance warranted, He could be downright stern. In other words, Jesus adapted Himself to the specific situation. So should the Christian counselor. (See 1 Thess. 5:14.)

Reflecting Christ's ministry, the hallmarks of Christian counseling are kindness and gentleness (2 Cor. 1:3–4; 10:1; Gal. 6:1; 1 Thess. 2:7, 11; 2 Tim. 2:24; Titus 3:2). The most obvious sign of Christ's ministering to and through the Christian counselor will be the love he shows to his clients. Remember that love is a major emphasis of Scripture: "Though I speak with the tongues of men and of angels, and have not charity, I am become as sounding brass, or a tinkling cymbal" (1 Cor. 13:1, KJV); "But the fruit of the Spirit is love, joy, peace, longsuffering, gentleness, goodness, faith, meekness, temperance: against such there is no law" (Gal. 5:22–23, KJV).

The counselor's efforts to model a Christlike attitude will be evident from the initial contact through every aspect of the counseling process. By adopting a Christlike approach the counselor will be able to put the counselee at ease, establish rapport, set a tone of honesty for the interview, and show compassion, concern, and empathy. Such a counselor will be responsive to variations in the client's mood. He will be flexible in dealing with difficult situations (e.g., if the counselee refuses to talk or is obviously paranoid), avoid any show of great surprise, and maintain an appropriate level of eye contact. He will be sensitive to such seemingly small matters as the physical setting (e.g., the placement of the chairs) and his body position (he will lean slightly forward to demonstrate interest). The communication will be on a level the counselee can understand. The counselor who patterns his approach after Christ's will develop acute listening skills (James 1:19) and will be able to elicit pertinent information tactfully.

The Ability to Use Scripture

Scripture plays a crucial role in Christian counseling. By providing spiritual nourishment God's Word produces growth and healing in the counselee. The Christian counselor will employ the Bible with discernment, tact, and sensitivity. There is a variety of ways in which the counselor can use God's Word; for example, as a means of direct challenge and confrontation, or as a source of encouragement and positive reinforcement. The Bible also offers practical advice and numerous models of godly lives. Under appropriate circumstances the counselor might consider giving homework assignments (Bible study and/or memorization). Or he might help his client by pointing out passages which have been of special benefit in his own personal life. With experience the counselor will discover more and more ways in which to use the Bible.

We have seen that there are a number of requisites for successful Christian counseling. They include skill in obtaining data, the ability to formulate an approach suitable for the individual counselee, a Christlike attitude, and knowledge of how to use Scripture. The wise counselor will periodically evaluate himself and earnestly strive for improvement in those areas where he falls short.

8

Putting It All Together

The Holistic Nature of Man

It is our intent in this final chapter to reiterate the most vital concepts we have discussed. A recurrent note has been the complex nature of man. In counseling sessions the psychological dimension of problems is, of course, the most evident and must be dealt with. But spiritual aspects are of utmost importance, and physical factors may also be involved. The three dimensions are integrally related and continuously affect one another.

When Elijah was depressed, God took care of the needs of the whole man (1 Kings 19). In like manner the Christian counselor must deal with the psychological, physical, and spiritual dimensions of his clients. But his most basic concern must center around the spiritual. It is worth noting that our words *holy* and *healthy* can be traced back to the same Anglo-Saxon root (*hal*). Apparently there is a relationship between being holy and being healthy. Ministering to the spiritual aspect to produce a holy person can produce a healthy person.

Ministering to the spiritual dimension is most crucial in the case of those who have little or no personal relationship with God. As soon as possible the counselor must determine the answers to the following questions:

1. Does the counselee know Christ?
2. Does the counselee have an awareness of the truths contained in verses like Romans 3:23, Romans 6:23, and John 1:12? In other words, does he need to hear the simple plan of salvation?
3. Is the counselee in bondage and in need of the Word of God? Christ points to the solution: "And you shall know the

truth, and the truth shall make you free" (John 8:32, NASB).
Is the counselee spiritually immature and in need of
growing in Christ? In that case he should be encouraged to
follow the apostle Peter's advice: "Like newborn babes, long
for the pure milk of the word, that by it you may grow in
respect to salvation" (1 Peter 2:2, NASB).

The Christian counselor realizes that the solution to many of
his clients' problems lies in acquainting them with the fundamental truths of the Bible. When it comes to producing spiritual
health and growth, nothing can match nourishment from the
Word of God. This is a point often emphasized in the Bible. God
says that His Word is our life (Deut. 32:46–47). It brings success
(Josh. 1:8). The man who delights in God's law is healthy; in fact
he is like a fruit-bearing tree planted by the rivers of water (Ps.
1:2–3). Rejoicing at God's Word is like finding great spoil (Ps.
119:162). Man shall not live by bread alone, but by every word
that proceeds out of the mouth of God (Matt. 4:4). Christ said
His words are spirit and life (John 6:63). The apostle Paul com-
mended his hearers to the Word of God, which was able to build
them up (Acts 20:32). Scripture has been given by inspiration of
God, that the man of God may be perfect (2 Tim. 3:16–17). There
is a correlation between strength and the abiding presence of
God's Word (1 John 2:14). Perhaps Solomon summed it up best:

> My son, give attention to my words;
> Incline your ear to my sayings.
> Do not let them depart from your sight;
> Keep them in the midst of your heart.
> For they are life to those who find them,
> And health to all their whole body (Prov. 4:20–22, NASB).

The Christian counselor must be ever on the lookout for different ways and opportunities in which to use the Word of God
in counseling. He himself must enjoy the Word, and that enjoy-
ment must be evident to the counselee. Perhaps the greatest
need the counselee may have is for someone to communicate to
him how to find delight in the Word of God. Enjoying the Word
on a regular basis may be the solution to his problems.

One of the counselor's aims is to discover whether the counselee is involved in a specific sin and needs help in dealing with it. The counselee may need to be gently confronted (Gal. 6:1). He may need support and encouragement from others in the body of Christ so that he not be hardened through the deceitfulness of sin (Heb. 3:13). Or he may need to spend a regular time with the Word of God in order to ward off the temptation to sin (Ps. 119:9–11).

As the counselor seeks to help his clients particularly through the spiritual dimension, he must realize that there are some individuals whose problem is essentially physical or biochemical in nature (e.g., psychosis or endogenous depression). Such individuals may have to be referred to another professional. A client who appears to be suicidal should be referred for hospitalization. It is a grievous mistake to think that all problems can be treated by purely spiritual means. Here again we are reminded of the complex nature of man. How tragic it is when a family refuses to seek proper professional help for a physical or biochemical problem on the grounds that to do so would be unspiritual.

It is imperative to treat all the dimensions of man—spiritual, psychological, and physical. We offer as an example the case of a fifty-five-year-old man who was referred to us by his doctor. He had received good care over the years from several professionals, including his pastor and a psychiatrist. But in attempting to help him, no one had taken into account the fact that man is a complex being composed of several interacting dimensions. Our new patient felt desperate. He commented that it seemed God had given up on him.

We began by giving attention to the patient's physical problem. He had never received medical treatment for a biochemical depression from which he had suffered for many years. Once he was given proper medication for this condition, he became more objective regarding his spiritual and psychological state.

A chaplain was assigned to our patient to help him deal with his spiritual difficulties. The chaplain modeled a kind, gentle, Christlike attitude. Special efforts to create a relaxed atmosphere around the patient helped rid him of his long-standing perception of God as a strict, harsh disciplinarian whose chief joy lies in punishing men for their every mistake and misdeed.

Our patient was also given psychological insight into his unresolved bitterness and fear. Fellow counselees gave him support
and encouragement. He began to implement the insight he
received and to make appropriate behavioral changes. After one
month of intensive care he felt better than he had for fifteen
years. The point is simply this: the wise counselor is sensitive to
and able to work with the whole man!

An Appropriate Approach

In addition to an awareness of the holistic nature of man, the
Christian counselor must have both a broad knowledge of the
great variety of approaches which are available and a sensitivity
as to which approach is most suitable for each counselee. The
counselor will know when to offer support, whether in the form
of advice, comfort, encouragement, or education. He will know
when to provide insight, when to urge confession, when to give
positive verbal reinforcement. With some counselees a Christian
example after which they can model their own lives is called for;
others need to be educated to God's truths; still others can best
be helped by interaction with a group. Family counseling may
be desirable. Other possible approaches include direct confrontation and assertiveness training.

Obviously, flexibility is a requisite for successful Christian
counseling. There are times to be direct (Prov. 27:5–6); there are
times to be indirect (2 Sam. 12:1–7). There are times to confront;
there are times to encourage (1 Thess. 5:14). There are times to
speak; there are times to listen (Eccles. 3:7). Christ was stern at
times (Mark 10:14); He was ever so gentle at other times (Mark
10:16).

The Christian counselor must also have a wide knowledge of
Scripture and a flexibility in using it. Some passages in the Bible
are appropriate for dealing with past sins (1 John 1:9); others
focus on the present (Matt. 6:34); still others point toward the
future (John 14:1–3). Some verses concentrate on behavior (Gen.
4:6–7), others on feelings (witness the great variety of Christ's
emotions). The wise counselor will know just which Scripture
passages to utilize in a given situation.

A Christlike Attitude

Even more important than knowledge of and ability to use various counseling approaches is the modeling of a Christlike attitude. The counselee will identify with the counselor and attempt to follow the example he sets. Thus the counselor should be gentle and kind. "What is desirable in a man is his kindness" (Prov. 19:22a, NASB). Psychiatric research has found that successful counselors demonstrate nonpossessive warmth, empathy, and sincerity. The essence of a Christlike attitude is perhaps best captured by the word *love* (1 Cor. 13). The counselor who makes the effort to personify a Christlike attitude, cares for the needs of the whole man (physical and spiritual as well as psychological), can formulate a counseling approach suitable to the individual, and looks to God for guidance will be successful as he endeavors to restore his clients to health.

Select Bibliography

American Psychiatric Association. "Psychiatric Board Review Course." Cassette-tape series. Belmont, MA: McLean Facility for Continuing Education, 1977.

———. "Survey of Psychiatry." Cassette-tape series. New York: Audio-Visual Medical Marketing, 1980.

Arieti, Silvano, ed. *American Handbook of Psychiatry.* 6 vols. 2nd ed. New York: Basic Books, 1974.

Backus, Joe T., and Shannon, Robert F. "The Psychodynamics of Depression." *Journal of the Arkansas Medical Society* 1 (1973).

Carter, John D. "Secular and Sacred Models of Psychology and Religion." *Journal of Psychology and Theology* (1977): 197–208.

———. "Towards a Biblical Model of Counseling." *Journal of Psychology and Theology* (1980): 45–52.

Chatton, Milton, and Krupp, Marcus. *Current Medical Diagnosis and Treatment.* Los Altos, CA: Lange Medical Publications, 1981.

Crabb, Lawrence J., Jr. *Effective Biblical Counseling.* Grand Rapids: Zondervan, 1977.

Davis, John M., ed. *Depression: A Practical Approach.* New York: Medcom, 1974.

Diagnostic and Statistical Manual of Mental Disorders. 3rd ed. Washington, DC: American Psychiatric Association, 1978.

Eaton, Merrill T., and Peterson, Margaret H. *Psychiatry.* Flushing, NY: Medical Examination Publishing Company, 1969.

Frank, Jerome D. "Holistic Components of Illness and Healing." *Weekly Psychiatry Update Series* 2. Lesson 18. Princeton, NJ: Biomedia, 1978.

Freedman, Alfred, et al. *Modern Synopsis of Psychiatry.* Baltimore: Williams and Wilkins, 1972.

Good, Roger C. "Practical Reviews in Family Practice." Vol. 5, no. 3. Cassette tape. Birmingham, AL: Educational Reviews, 1980.

Herink, Richie, ed. *The Psychotherapy Handbook.* New York: New American Library, 1980.

Kaplan, Harold; Freedman, Alfred; and Sadock, Benjamin. *Comprehensive Textbook of Psychiatry.* 3 vols. 3rd ed. Baltimore: Williams and Wilkins, 1980.

Karaus, Toksoz B. "Psychotherapies: An Overview." *American Journal of Psychiatry* 134.8 (1977): 851–63.

Kolb, Lawrence C. *Modern Clinical Psychiatry.* 8th ed. Philadelphia: W. B. Saunders, 1973.

Lewis C. S. *The Screwtape Letters.* New York: Macmillan, 1972.

Merrell-National Laboratories. "Depression Notes." Cassette-tape series. Cincinnati: Merrell-National Laboratories, 1977.

Minirth, Frank B. *Christian Psychiatry.* Old Tappan, NJ: Fleming H. Revell, 1977.

———, and Meier, Paul D. *Happiness Is a Choice.* Grand Rapids: Baker, 1978.

———, et al. *The Workaholic and His Family: An Inside Look.* Grand Rapids: Baker, 1981.

Morris, Charles. *Psychology: An Introduction.* New York: Appleton-Century-Crofts, 1973.

Nelson, Melvin R. "The Psychology of Spiritual Conflict." *Journal of Psychology and Theology* 1 (1976): 34–41.

Patch, Vernon D., and Solomon, Philip, eds. *Handbook of Psychiatry.* 3rd ed. Los Altos, CA: Lange Medical Publications, 1974.

Robinson, Haddon, ed. "Whole-Person Medicine." *Christian Medical Society Journal* 11 (1981).

Schaeffer, Francis A. *True Spirituality.* Wheaton, IL: Tyndale, 1971.